TEN YEARS AND CHANGE

A Liberal Boyhood in Minnesota

MICHAEL P. AMRAM

Wisdom Editions
Minneapolis, Minnesota

Wisdom Editions
Minneapolis

FIRST EDITION MAY 2017
TEN YEARS AND CHANGE: A Liberal Boyhood in Minnesota.

Printed in the United States of America.
10 9 8 7 6 5 4 3 2 1

Cover and interior design: Gary Lindberg

ISBN: 978-1-939548-71-9

To my parents who seized the moments to teach,
to dissident Democrats who proved what minorities may reach

Contents

TEN YEARS AND CHANGE

A Liberal Boyhood in Minnesota

MICHAEL P. AMRAM

Prologue

Beginning in 1882, a series of events occurred which culminated in the formation of the Democratic Farmer-Labor Party. An Irish immigrant named John Fitzpatrick came to the United States and settled in Chicago. He found work as a horseshoer, and eventually he joined the International Journeyman Horseshoers' Union. Over the next three decades he served as treasurer, business agent and finally president of the Chicago local IJHU. Fitzpatrick was often a delegate to union conventions and a representative to the American Federation of Labor. Using this connection, in 1906 he organized the Chicago Federation of Labor. By 1919—in the wake of the First World War—Fitzpatrick had persuaded many state-level labor parties to form one national labor party. One of its primary objectives was to unify the efforts of the country's industrial workers with the farmers movement and the cooperative movement. A modern Farmer-Labor Party had first emerged in Minnesota in 1918 when America's entry into the First World War caused economic dislocation, and agricultural prices and workers' wages were affected. Inflation in retail prices caused an imbalance in the US economy.

A group of progressives, known as The Committee of 48, was an agrarian political association. They formed in 1919 and set out to create a new party for social reform. In 1920, without success, progressive members of the committee attempted to create a third party. The group—often referred to simply as "Forty-

Eighters"—went on to become a key constituent in the Conference for Progressive Political Action. The Committee of 48—referring to the existing forty-eight United States—merged with the Labor Party in July 1920 to form a federated Farmer-Labor Party. Finally, in 1944, the Democratic Party merged with the Farmer-Labor Party to form the Democratic Farmer-Labor Party (DFL). The merger came about through the efforts of Hubert Humphrey (thirty-fifth mayor of Minneapolis) and Elmer Benson (the state's twenty-fourth governor).

As a memoir of Minnesota's anti-war movement through the years 1965-1975, the progression of gender and racial equality and the Vietnam War's impact on how America changed, this book intertwines politics with growing up during those years. I wanted to commend many for their past social awareness. They left a lesson in history about the power of people, the power of one state and the power of one community. *Ten Years and Change: A Liberal Boyhood in Minnesota* focuses on the band of dissenters in the DFL Party. It is a testimonial to the tenacity and political acumen of the DFL's anti-war efforts. I reference the legacy left by many who attempted to create a constituency within the establishment whose sole purpose was to permanently end military operations in Southeast Asia. A minority of the DFL challenged the Johnson-Humphrey administration because they were dissatisfied with the administration's foreign policy. They supported Minnesota Senator Eugene McCarthy in his effort to seek the 1968 Democratic presidential nomination as an anti-war candidate.

When I began this project in 2014, I considered America's recent military history. I thought of George W. Bush's war in Iraq and its specious conception. Soldiers often served multiple tours of duty, and a draft of troops was thinly veiled. A stop-loss policy facilitated involuntary military service. In 2004 Senator John Kerry, in a presidential campaign speech, dubbed it a "backdoor draft." Soldiers interviewed in the Iraqi desert said they had no idea why they were there and what the parameters for victory were. Then, realizing the parallels—a deja vu tapis—I allowed myself to regress to the atmosphere that nurtured my childhood. I envisioned the years 1965 to 1975 and tried to pin down when I first had any real sense, or enough curiosity to reason, what was occurring in our house and in the world beyond its door. I thought about the short-term effects of what was being done to expedite the end of the war in Vietnam. I considered what efforts were being made—efforts discussed around our dining room table—to end what I perceived as a terrible thing happening in a place called Vietnam. They were not the random acts of civil disobedience the first amendment allows us. The processes of disobedience followed an established set of rules and bylaws. If a band of hippies could not end the war by lying in the path of troop trains, a minority of Democrats who got "clean for Gene" would present themselves as a constituency to those with the power to end it.

I spoke with former McCarthy supporters and delegates, and their faces twisted from intrusive light. My questions about bittersweet times commenced an ambivalence. I dug at repressed corners of their minds, and they responded with a hesitant fondness. With a precarious laugh, they replied, making no discernible connection to today's political climate. What they had done was isolated. It was an action necessitated by an unmitigated war each belligerent refused to end. It was clear to me that the efforts made by the DFL dissidents were isolated incidents. The same tactic applied to unseat an incumbent president to end a war was not likely to happen again. The year 1968—three years after Johnson began bombing North Vietnam—stood out in the ten year period I examine. It was filled with upsets, feelings of hopelessness, and unrequited calls for peace.

One thing became abundantly clear to me as I researched the war protests, race riots, lies, and deception. America is not always number one, nor should anyone be made to feel it has to be. Sometimes number two has to suffice. In history there have been instances when the notion that the United States of America is infallible must be denied. It is the America that was fabricated and presented to sell things like unconstitutional wars and police actions.

In *Ten Years and Change: A Liberal Boyhood in Minnesota,* I reference a small group of Democrats who stepped out of the mainstream to end an unconstitutional and immoral war. But they did much more. They presented themselves for the 'teachable moments,' the times opportunity knocked in those ten years to offer change; the times when minds were fertile for seeds of ideas to be planted for the future betterment of racial and gender equality. The people I watched in the DFL when I was young were not afraid to point out that America did not always win or follow the right path to the future. They went against the Johnson policies that kept us in Vietnam out of a misguided sense of patriotism. They taught me that justice was not only for white, affluent men. They saw to it that human rights were withheld from no one. As one who grew up watching metaphorical flowers pollenate gun barrels, I like to think all the effort to make a peaceful, just and equal future affected society positively.

hawks uproot
the earth— talon's
till buries sparse
the seeds they sow…

their necks are hung
with wreaths
of flowers at
Arlington-
circles of hope that
peace will grow…

Chapter One

Several Small Steps

A gas station's sign disappeared into the night sky stirring northern Minnesota's stars like a divining rod. A maroon station wagon jostled along County Road 10. The asphalt was riddled with potholes and bucked the wagon forward. I sat unrestrained and free to move in the back deck of that wagon watching the silhouettes of my sister and myself in the dark desolate hills it had overcome.

In 1969 I spent my first summer in cabin land. I glanced at the front of the car intermittently, hoping to catch a glimpse of the soft greens of the dashboard lights. My dad always found bonus adventures at the end of the day. It was a night like any other Sunday night in Bay Lake Township. I felt our station wagon veer off the road. Its tires crunched, and my dad turned into the store's small gravely parking lot. The sound of the keys brushing the steering column went through the car. With the engine off the car coasted to a stop, instinctively maneuvering around two faded gas pumps. Our heads popped up over the backseat. Dad sat and looked up at the moon. Four days earlier, on July 16, a Saturn V rocket had launched Edwin Aldrin Jr., Michael Collins, and Neil Armstrong into space.

"Michael, Susan, I think you will want to stay awake for this."

I opened the car door and listened to crickets keeping rhythm for the night. A fallout of heat disheveled me more. It had been an eighty-six-degree day, and tepid thermals of warmth caught errant breezes. Something out of the ordinary—something remote to the average Sunday night—was on my dad's radar. Not often were we allowed to stay up this late. The four of us walked toward the store, following a fluorescent light that led the night through a screen door. We ushered in cool to hear it slam with a hollow sound of vacancy. Customer bells tinkled in resonance. We listened to minnow tanks humming, patiently waiting for tomorrow's net to be dipped. Green-hued bubbles streamed in perfect lines like tiny tendered orbs. The night crawlers in the store had an earthy smell that blended with sweeter smells of bubble gum and waffle cones.

Understated, at the back of the store, was a room. A barroom full of anglers and iron rangers sat in anticipation of the moon landing's broadcast. Soon I climbed on a stool and surveyed the television screen. The television crackled, and Walter Cronkite's face came into view. It was black and white, hazy and the horizontals struggled to escape the vertical lines' hold. The man who delivered news about war every night narrated a replay of the Apollo 11 capsule setting down on the moon at 8:18 p.m. Universal Coordinated Time (UTC). The lunar module bounced in gravity's absence, rocking for several minutes before settling on mechanical feet. The barroom sighed. Weather-worn shoot-from-the-hip iron rangers were moved to mask the anticipation their normal expressionless faces revealed. They waited—with gritted teeth—for the small module to depressurize. I glanced around the bar and saw them looking and nodding at each other. People united for the moment with whomever was near.

Six hours lagged in the dingy bar. The consciousness of ordinary people was connected. Anglers told their tales that, in light of recent events, seemed insignificant. Summer cabin dwellers sat in their happy places and grinned. They were so proud to not be so earth-bound that they missed seeing the landing in the comfort of their city home. My sister and I grew restless. As with many opportunities to see the world's triumphs and defeats that decade, my parents knew this was something we needed to see. They always knew what moments were worth teaching and superseded their natural parental instincts. Finally, a ladder dropped from the module following Houston's directives. After several seconds, Neil Armstrong responded "Houston, Tranquility Base here. The Eagle has landed." Cheers went around the bar once again. At 02:56, July 21, mission commander Armstrong began the descent down the module's nine-rung ladder to the lunar surface. Armstrong knew he was a poet whose words would echo into history. "That's one small step for man... one giant leap for mankind," he proclaimed as he broke away from the ladder. People cheered once more in the back of White Hawk. I imagined anywhere in the world, perhaps in Vietnam, people cheered. Cronkite took off his glasses and paused in pride and disbelief. It was a moment of humility. During a speech seven years earlier, President Kennedy had vowed to put a man on the moon by the decade's end. That was right on schedule. We had put a human on the moon before the Russians. All rivalries aside, for those hours that we spent in the back of a general store, I like to think of the world pausing from its current path of destruction to consider its future.

Ψ

Richfield, Minnesota borders Minneapolis to the south. In 1968 it was situated in the state's third congressional district within Hennepin County. At the time the county's DFL chairwoman was Barbara Amram, my mother. Much earlier she'd become involved in WILPF (Woman's International League for Peace and Freedom). The group worked to bring together women of different political views and philosophical and religious backgrounds. One of its missions was to study and expose the causes of war and work toward a permanent peace.

Mom's early work in the WILPF.
Photo courtesy of the *Richfield Sun*.

An example of carrying out that mission took place in 1963. Amram and fellow WILPH member Medora Petersen traveled to Washington, DC. Their sole purpose was to lobby for their senator's—Eugene McCarthy—vote and political actions to end the war in Vietnam. The year was pivotal with regards to America's involvement in the war.

Ψ

Early in November of 1963, after the removal of corrupt South Vietnamese dictator—and US ally—Ngô Đình Diêm, the war escalated. President Kennedy and his brother, Attorney General Robert Kennedy, contributed to actions that led to the removal of Diêm. "It's better if you don't have him, but you have to have somebody who can win the war, and who is that?"[1] The "who"

Robert Kennedy spoke of was never supplied. The United States, in an effort to win the war against the NLF (National Liberation Front), or Viet Cong, and North Vietnam, destroyed large parts of Vietnam.

Diêm was the victim of a coup designed by a military revolutionary council. It was made up of ARVN (Army of the Republic of Vietnam) leaders, one of whom was General Duong Văn Minh. Lieutenant Colonial Lucien Conein, a CIA operative, was functioning as a liaison between the US Embassy and the ARVN generals. In early October, a meeting was held at Tân Son Nhât airport in Ho Chi Minh City. Conein met with General Duong Văn Minh to discuss the role of the US in the coup. Conein arrived with a message from the White House claiming a US policy of non-intervention. The intent to remain neutral was later reiterated through US Ambassador Henry Cabot Lodge, Jr. His assurances, though, were shrouded in secrecy,[2] and on November 1, 1963, General Minh and his conspirators toppled Diêm's regime in a swift coup. Diêm was offered exile if he surrendered. The unseated president escaped to a church. He was eventually found and assassinated.

Ψ

My earliest recollections—of really anything in life—take the shape of jack-o'-lantern (Chinese lantern) plants. My mom grew them at our home in Richfield for WILPF fundraisers. They were put in vases to bring to the sale. The 'lanterns' hung limply from thin stems and inside outlined the tiny berries that sat perched in pyramid-shaped orange crackly casings. She also grew money plants to sell. They were called money plants because, when they dried, the leaves resembled coins.

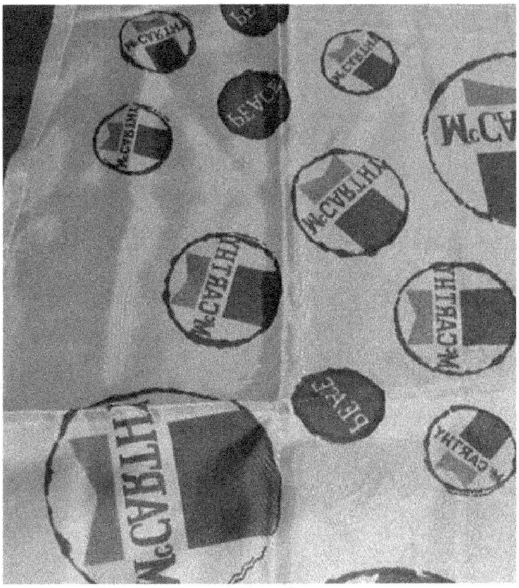

Scarf my mom wore

When I was two years and ten months old, Minnesota Senator Eugene McCarthy agreed to be the anti-war candidate who would oppose the hawkish Johnson administration for the Democratic nomination in the 1968 presidential election. I saw McCarthy emblazoned on blue and white buttons, stickers and scarves. Logistically, I was close to politics almost from my beginning. I was attending a nursery school at a YMCA located near the DFL headquarters in Minneapolis. My mom dropped me off there on her way to work as chairwoman in the building located on the 1600 block of Hennepin Avenue. Fred Amram, my father, talked to potential McCarthy supporters in a crowded, smoky basement room of the Richfield Bank down the street from our house. He told about a trip he and my mom had made to Germany in 1960. He recalled their visit to Dachau, the concentration camp built in the city in 1933. They were staying at a bed and breakfast in Munich, nine miles southeast of the camp. The proprietors of the B&B were asked about their memories of being located close to the camp. So nothing was lost in translation, Amram spoke in German—his native language—to his hosts as he described the crematoria. He asked whether they'd seen "black smoke twenty-four hours each day." He wanted to know whether they noticed ashes on their windowsills. They answered his questions. They truly believed that the smoke and ashes had come from a factory.

The gross analogy was made in hopes of bringing people to action. A parallel was there. The end result of each conflagration was the same: mass eradication of human life. For the German B&B owners in the 1930s, the atrocities had occurred in close proximity. For the audience in the bank basement, they were happening on the other side of the world. At Dachau, decisions to send people to certain death had been made only nine miles away, every day. All over America decisions to send young men, against their will, around the world to a possible death, dismemberment or lasting trauma disorders were made at induction centers and draft boards. The abrogating of each established order tested a consensus's moral conscience. By the end of his talk, the speech sign-up sheets started accumulating names.

McCarthy's anti-war philosophy appealed to many Catholics, and Amram made several visits to The Academy of the Holy Angels in Richfield. He taught the nuns the political process. The sisters learned the process of caucusing and, in turn, steered him to other enclaves of priests and nuns. He traveled around Minnesota for months and instructed clergy and church groups on caucus procedures. He visited St. Cloud, Minnesota with Don Fraser (US Representative from Minnesota's Fifth District). They worked as a team. Fraser briefed the groups on the pertinent issues and raised their awareness. Amram then taught the political process to enlighten the Catholic communities. Forrest Harris (Fifth District DFL Vice Chairman) occasionally accompanied Amram. The impromptu teach-ins worked well, and the nuns often ran for delegate seats to the senate district convention, sometimes outvoting the Humphrey delegates. They dressed in their habits and filled the front rows at the senate convention.

The dissenters in the DFL party all risked something, some more than others. Party officers and elected officials feared the lasting stigma of trying to unseat an incumbent president. McCarthy Democrats aimed to shield strategies from the Johnson-Humphrey Democrats, and some of their meetings were held in places removed from the DFL Party. One meeting took place in what was thought to be a private area in a shopping center in the neighboring city of Edina. The room was not private, and business went on as the meeting proceeded. The most loyal DFL members were very nervous. A few had mixed feelings about what they were doing. Those feelings permeated the meetings.

Chapter Two

Contraindicates

After the Chinese Communists defeated the French in the First Indochina War, a power struggle began in Vietnam. President Eisenhower sent advisors to train armies in the southern part of Vietnam (a treaty signed in 1954 by the French and the Chinese Communists had divided Vietnam at the seventeenth parallel).

In spite of Eisenhower's advice to keep an eye on Laos and Vietnam, Europe and Latin America "loomed larger than Asia"[1] in Kennedy's sight. In his inaugural address, Kennedy pledged to meet any hardship and "support any friend." He vowed that the United States would oppose any enemy and assured America of the survival of liberty.

Fifty thousand US troops remained in Korea in 1961. Kennedy did little to deviate from the Cold War policies set in place by Truman and Eisenhower. The three major issues that arose during his administration that had to be dealt with were the boondoggled Bay of Pigs Invasion, the erection of the Berlin Wall and a negotiated settlement between pro-Western Laos and the Communist movement called Pathet Lao. The three crises made the president fearful of irreparable damage to US credibility as a powerful nation. As a result, he sent military and financial aid to sustain the army of Ngô Đình Diêm, South Vietnam's president.

Toward the end of 1963 there were fifteen thousand soldiers in Vietnam acting as military advisors. Kennedy had greatly increased economic aid to South Vietnam. When Lyndon Johnson assumed the presidency he was careful not to upset policies that had been set in place. His approval rating remained high, and for six months 75 percent of America supported him. On July 2, 1964 he signed a civil rights act outlawing racial discrimination. Johnson easily defeated Republican Barry Goldwater in the presidential election with the widest margin—486 Electoral votes to 52—in American politics.[2] However, he inherited an illegitimate war. His predecessors—chiefly Eisenhower—had made promises to South Vietnam which he felt compelled to keep. Communist forces in North Vietnam were advancing on the army of the South. Feeling pressure to protect South Vietnam, the president took offensive actions early in 1965. Plans were approved for a sustained bombing operation on the Republic of North Vietnam by US air and naval forces. The 1964 Gulf of Tonkin Resolution provided Johnson with the leverage he needed to take offensive military action. In early March, F-105 Thunder Chiefs rained bombs over jungles. They burned brightly, engulfing in flames like Roman candles from the petroleum-based gelling agent napalm tearing through them. They also tore through innocent people in their path. Johnson's high rating began a steady decline and the anti-war movement in America grew like a wildfire.

Ψ

In the early 1960s the student body at the University of Minnesota campus in Minneapolis did not put political discussion of the conflict in Vietnam high on its agenda. Dennis Wadley reported for the university's newspaper the *Minnesota Daily*. A rally protesting the Cuban Missile Crisis crowded the university's Coffman Union in 1962. Students questioned Kennedy's decision to confront Khrushchev. They threw tomatoes when a radical organizer of the protest was hanged in effigy and the U of M witnessed hysteria never before seen at such levels. The actions that day were primal and the level of disobedience the faculty could tolerate was tested.

Gradually, the conflict in Vietnam made its way up on the agendas of student body presidents. Johnson's policies were widely criticized and documented in the university's newspaper, the *Minnesota Daily:*

The Minnesota Daily

World's largest college newspaper

> Minneapolis, St. Paul, Minn. Tuesday, August 11, 1964
> "America's moral posture in Vietnam-an indictment of hypocrisy"

Another headline that year in November simply stated, "Let's get out of Vietnam." It was not a suggestion or a topic open for debate. It was a statement of the mentality a growing number of young adults had. Students around the country were publicly opposing the war on college campuses. The University of Minnesota campuses in Minneapolis and Duluth were home to many protests and demonstrations.

The city of Minneapolis is divided into thirteen political wards. The sixth ward skirted Minneapolis's eastern edge. The area was old, and many houses were in need of repair. The draft for the war resulted in a surge of college enrollment, and space at the University was tight. Students moved into dilapidated duplexes, or they rented rooms above stores. They had their own DFL chapter called the YDFL (Young Democratic-Farmer Labor).

In the fall of 1964 a second-year law student enrolled at the University of Minnesota. Vance Opperman arrived from Iowa's Grinnell College where he'd earned a reputation as an activist and leader of the student body. In Minneapolis he began a campaign to get Congressman Don Fraser reelected. In 1966, Opperman led the YDFL's "Sixth Ward Club" to the DFL state senate committee. The war in Vietnam was now a topic on most agendas, and a resolution to go forward and press the Johnson administration to get out of Southeast Asia was set before the Sixth Ward. At a meeting held to present the resolution, university professors were the first to speak. Most opposed the administration's war policies. When the debate concluded, the floor was open to resolutions. Howard Kaibel (a law student and student body president) informally spoke from the edge of a table. He was candid about the war and sensibilities toward it.

"Those of us here with a moral point of view already know how we're going to vote on this resolution,"[3] he said.

He continued and the implied disparagement of the 'immoralists' present leaked from his words in indiscriminate clusters. The anti-war resolution was multiple pages of single-spaced lines. Some articles spoke of the federal income tax surcharge that could be imposed for being undemocratic. Not everyone in the DFL equated ending the war with supporting an anti-war candidate. The majority, however, felt that to vote against the war, the endorsement of such a candidate was imperative.

Students from the Sixth Ward attended the 1966 DFL state convention, where a motion was made to restrict voting to those over twenty-one, then the legal US voting age. After much fierce debate, the motion failed. It was modified to allow anyone over eighteen, the draft age, to vote and was passed. The U of M's student body took over the Sixth Ward DFL club and elected Opperman chairman. The war in Vietnam was at the top of the political agenda at the university for much of 1966 with one exception.

At the DFL state convention, incumbent governor Karl Rolvaag failed to get the endorsement of his party. The DFL chose to endorse his Lieutenant Governor Alexander "Sandy" Keith. Keith had a smooth and articulate speaking style which appealed to students. An important issue was academic freedom on the university campus. Rolvaag tended to be more moderate while Keith publicly questioned the direction the university board was going with regard to academic freedom. His campaign advisors tried to quiet him, fearing damage to his bid for the governorship. The DFL state central committee fiercely contested the issue. Rolvaag pleaded, "Let the people decide!" as he entered the DFL's primary race. The incumbent governor soundly defeated Keith, but lost in the November election to Republican Harold LeVander.

Ψ

In March of 1966 a protest in Minneapolis against the draft took place at the First Unitarian Society in observance of the International Day of Protest. Peaceful marchers lined three blocks of downtown Minneapolis. Sixty-five University of Minnesota professors, artists and doctors signed a petition for the cause. The June 7 *New York Times* featured the protest and the signatures. A story about an anti-war rally in August appeared in the *Minneapolis Tribune*. The paper's August 7, 1966 edition described the event:

> "The marchers ranged from professors to hairy peacenik types. There were babes in arms, strollers and wagons, and in one case, a car seat slung over a mother's back."[4]

Anti-war lectures dubbed "teach-ins" and "truth-outs" were held in various cities. They were general education forums on any current contentious issue. The largest anti-war teach-in occurred May 21-23, 1965 at the University of California, Berkeley. It was organized by the Vietnam Day Committee. Among its organizers was alumnus Jerry Rubin. A political science professor had prepared a speech defending President Johnson's handling of the war, but he was vastly outnumbered by Johnson's critics and, in the end, declined to speak.

In 1969 an anti-war teach-in took place on the U of M campus. It was part of the October 15 "Vietnam Moratorium Day." Nearly half of the university's forty-thousand-member student body attended the various lectures. Ten thousand people gathered in downtown Minneapolis that morning. By nine a.m., Washington Avenue was filled with demonstrators. They traversed a footbridge and filed peacefully into the plaza in front of the university's Coffman Union. Later that afternoon, the group marched to the armed forces induction center a mile from campus. Around two p.m., a small group of dissenters approached the Nicollet Mall intent on challenging authority. Bill Tilton, the president of the Minnesota Student Association, was nervous and tried to persuade the group against any malicious intent. A witness described Tilton's actions that day:

> "Up and down the mall he roamed, pleading: 'Let's work for peace… break it up. You're not doing any good for peace that way. This is what Stenvig (Mayor of Minneapolis) wants you to do.'"[5]

Similar rallies and anti-war activities were held that day on the Augsburg College and Hamline University campuses in the Twin Cities. Minnesota Representative Donald Fraser and Minnesota Supreme Court Justice James Otis gave speeches. Julian Bond and Walter Mondale spoke at Macalester College in St. Paul. Bond, then a Georgia state representative, had been active in the civil rights movement and, later, various committees opposing the war. Mondale, a US senator representing Minnesota, received a standing ovation when he publicly stated his position on the war. The speech confirmed his non-complicity with the administration in regard to the war.

Ψ

Allard Lowenstein was an activist and one-term congressman from New York, representing Nassau County's Fifth District from 1969 to 1971. When the National Student Association (NSA) convened in Washington, DC, on August 15, 1967, Lowenstein and Curtis Gans, a political activist and voting pattern analyst, began a "dump Johnson" movement. The campaign was an effort to build opposition to the renomination of the president. The movement was regarded as highly quixotic and impractical. Gans and Lowenstein convinced a minority of Democrats that Lyndon Johnson no longer espoused the ideals of Roosevelt, Truman or Kennedy.

In one week, during October of 1967, in eighteen cities, over twelve thousand young men either turned in or burned their draft cards. It was one of the acts that took place in what were known as the Stop the Draft Week Protests. Lowenstein warned that the anti-Vietnam War movement was too often referred to as a protest. He advised students like Kaibel and Opperman to remember that they were trying to convince our society they were the majority. Lowenstein was determined to prove to Lyndon Jonson the difficulty of continuing his bid for his party's nomination.

In 1966 there were only fifteen or twenty senators who had made any kind of firm commitment to opposing the war. During a phone call on February 1, Senator McCarthy expressed his concerns about the war to Johnson. He told the senator that they were legitimate concerns, adding that he understood the basis for them. McCarthy's concerns were vacuous to the president, and clearly the Senate was powerless to change executive policy for the war. He decided the only way the administration was going to significantly alter its policies in Southeast Asia was to make the war an issue in the 1968 campaign.

Ψ

Eugene Joseph McCarthy came from the small central Minnesota town of Watkins. He was the son of a devoutly Catholic mother and a strong-willed father of Irish descent. Historians have said

McCarthy was "peat bog Irish," conjuring the image of an Irishman staring into a peat bog thinking deeply. During his years attending St. Anthony's, a Catholic school in Watkins, the monks at St. John's Abbey and University had a strong influence on him. Before leaving the monastery, McCarthy spent nine months as a novice Benedictine monk. According to historian Dominic Sandbrook, McCarthy claimed Catholicism was the single most important thing in his life. In 1932 he graduated from St. John's University in Collegeville, Minnesota and went on to earn a graduate degree from the University of Minnesota.

From 1949 to 1959 he represented Minnesota's Fourth Congressional District. After being elected to the US Senate he supported Adlai Stevenson in the 1960 presidential campaign. Stevenson sought the Democratic nomination opposing Kennedy. In a speech nominating Stevenson he warned people not to reject a man who made him proud to be a Democrat. The first-term senator took the opportunity to bolster his own credibility. He said, "I'm twice as liberal as Hubert Humphrey, twice as intelligent as [Senator] Stuart Symington (D-MO), and twice as Catholic as Jack Kennedy."[6] In the 1964 presidential race McCarthy was considered as a running mate for Lyndon Johnson, along with Senator Thomas Dodd (D-CT) and fellow Minnesota Senator Hubert Humphrey.

As New Hampshire thawed, young voters "cleaned for Gene." The 1968 primary race in the Granite State saw a first. In general, the younger generation had not been particularly active in politics. McCarthy's anti-war philosophy resonated with the young. It was felt that his ideas would be embraced more readily if they came from a clean-cut individual. Unkempt minions cleaned for him. College students sheared their hair and shaved their beards. Educations were given sabbaticals while students voraciously campaigned for Gene though the spring and summer of 1968. On the Minneapolis and Duluth campuses of the U of M, groups like SDS (Student Democratic Society) were being formed. A goal was to turn ordinary people against the war. Academics, doctors, lawyers—those who were already in successful careers needed to be moved by young people to get involved in the anti-war movement. In 1966, 80 percent of Americans supported our involvement in Southeast Asia; by 1969 only 20 percent of Americans supported Johnson's foreign policies.

Early in 1967, Senator Eugene McCarthy and Congressman Joseph Karth were quoted in the *St. Paul Pioneer Press.* They answered questions regarding US involvement in Vietnam. Karth asserted that the American bombing of North Vietnam had to stop and that the United Nations needed to be more aggressive in its protection of South Vietnam. He pointed out that, despite what the administration liked to claim, the bombing efforts of the US had done little to stem the migration of Vietnamese to the south. In the same edition of the paper, McCarthy contemplated the idea of victory in Vietnam. He questioned if a victory would be proportionate to what it had cost. He queried whether a US victory would provide a better life for the South Vietnamese. Later that spring, McCarthy spoke in Minneapolis to elaborate on the ideas he had expressed in the *Pioneer Press* article. He urged a cessation of bombing and a partial withdrawal of our troops in Southeast Asia. He thought the war policies of the Johnson administration were highly questionable and likely to fail any objective investigation. Being a long-time friend of Vice President Humphrey, the senator's critical words came as a shock to many.

One evening, in the fall of 1967, a dinner party convened. Guests dressed casually and arrived in accordance of the appointed time. Forrest Harris, DFL vice chairman, led the meeting:

"... in the summer of 1967, a man by the name of Bill Smith came to talk about organizing a group he called 'Dissident Democrats' to express displeasure with the deepening of the war. ... Then there began a series of small meetings, often with Maurice Visscher (head of physiology at the University of Minnesota), and finally I attended a dinner meeting where it was decided that we should organize a protest movement."[7]

The dinner party was a ruse. The meeting's true purpose was to discuss stepping out of the DFL Party's mainstream. In addition to Visscher, the guest list included Donald Heffernan (a Minneapolis lawyer), Esther Wattenberg (a U of M professor of social work), Alpha Smaby (a member of the state House of Representatives), and Kaibel. Visscher called the meeting to order and explained the consequences of the group's actions. He cautioned the members about the rigorous public scrutiny they may encounter. He said that anyone forming a group opposing the established political party had best be prepared for anything the media might ferret out about them.

Smaby risked her reputation. Harris was reluctant to dissent and initially backed away from the idea Smith brought up that summer. He thought they'd be seen as traitors and, as fifth district vice chairman, he felt a sense of responsibility to his party. Kaibel reminded the members that his previous attempt in Washington, DC to change the course of action in Southeast Asia had been a failure. By the end of the meeting, it was unanimously decided that a committee be formed to guide Democrats toward the goal of 'dumping' the incumbent president. DFL members prepared for the mutinous path they had chosen. Many present at the meeting had worked for Humphrey when he was a Minneapolis mayor and US Senator. Humphrey's accolades for his past defenses of civil rights were lauded by all. However, it was also unanimously felt that distancing themselves from the Johnson-Humphrey policy in Vietnam was critical.

Later that fall, at a meeting of the Sixth Ward Club, a resolution was proposed for the immediate and unmitigated withdrawal of troops from Vietnam. It was verbose and flouted a policy which stated new resolutions must have prior notification. Wattenberg and Smaby were the first to vote on the resolution. Smaby mentioned the dinner party and, to bolster the credibility of the resolution, Wattenberg mentioned the messianic arrival of Allard Lowenstein.

The war resolution was adopted. It was recognized as the first overt act in opposition of Lyndon Johnson's Vietnam policy to be made public. A reporter for the *Minneapolis Star,* Ted Smebakken, pointed out in his article that a small number of Republicans now also favored withdrawal from Vietnam.

"We submit the proposition that American prestige is solid enough to weather a withdrawal from Vietnam, and we should be formulating plans to do so forthwith,"[8] Smebakken wrote, beginning his article with an excerpt from the *Republican Workshop Bulletin.* The *Bulletin* article had been edited by a noted St. Paul Republican and was the first from that party publicly criticizing the administration's efforts in Vietnam. Opposition to the war had reached a boiling point, with less than half the nation favoring Johnson's foreign policies.

In 1968, two issues began to add to the pressure on the president. Each stoked the fires of the anti-war movement. On January 30, the North Vietnamese and the Viet Cong launched an attack on South Vietnamese targets. The offensive action was in coordination with the lunar new year, or Tet, observance. Heavy casualties were sustained by the US and South Vietnamese. Ho Chi Minh and other leaders in Hanoi launched the offensive hoping it would give them a decisive victory and put an end to the quagmire that threatened to envelop military leaders on both sides.

A movement to repeal the Gulf of Tonkin resolution had been simmering since 1967. Its critics had almost immediately moved to repeal the 1964 resolution they said gave Johnson a blank check to escalate a war.

Ψ

The allegation of the 1964 attack justified retaliation, fire power and troop surges. Falsified information funneled into the White House following the attack. It was later found that on Aug. 4, Hanoi's naval forces were only salvaging damaged boats. Privately, the president was heard to say, "For all I know, our navy was shooting at whales out there."[9] On August 5, the president authorized the retaliatory strike Operation Pierce Arrow. Two days later, Congress approved the Gulf of Tonkin Resolution. It asserted that Congress condoned and supported any retributory acts made by the president. As commander in chief, the president could "take all necessary measures" to repel armed aggression against the US "and to prevent further aggression…"[10]

Provocation is a dual-edged sword, and when progressions are invoked the cause for vindication is generally not questioned. However, if there is any doubt of provocation, any line of defense or offense is highly questionable. The initial attacks in the Gulf of Tonkin were not unprovoked. Hanoi saw America as puppets of South Vietnam. America had its own puppet forces that were claimed to have shelled two of North Vietnam's coastal islands. During the night of July 30 to 31, the small islands of Hon Me and Hon Nieu were attacked. US press releases denied knowledge of the incident. In the days that followed, behind closed doors, Secretary of State Dean Rusk and Secretary of Defense Robert McNamara did acknowledge the attacks. They cautioned, however, that technically they could not be seen as US provocations for counter-attacks by North Vietnam. As proxies, the US could have said the entire operation was run by the South Vietnamese navy. The claim would have been false, as South Vietnam had little, if any, part in the raids on the islands. The operations were completely the work of the US.

Johnson's offensive action—Operation Pierce Arrow—stood justified. The House of Representatives had unanimously approved the Gulf of Tonkin Resolution. The Senate found only two objectors in ninety: Senators Morse (D-OR) and Ernest Gruening (D-AK). Many senators, including George McGovern (D-SD), Albert Gore, Sr. (D-TN), and John Sherman Cooper (R-KY), expressed concern that the resolution's language was too broad. It allowed Johnson to launch direct combat involvement, including the deployment of ground troops. Assurances came from Senator J. William Fulbright (D-AR) that there was no consideration in the Johnson administration of using the resolution as a means to change the American role in the war. He insisted he had "no doubt that the president will consult with Congress in case a major change in present policy becomes necessary." Fulbright had sponsored and voted for the resolution, but his assurance was unfounded. He had been duped and unwittingly misled the Senate. He later denounced the resolution, saying a "wider war" had been sought. "Many senators who accepted the Gulf of Tonkin Resolution without question may well have not done so had they foreseen that it was subsequently interpreted as a sweeping congressional endorsement for the conduct of a large-scale war in Asia," he wrote.

In 1964, Johnson had secretly promised the Hanoi regime an escalated war on North Vietnam, saying he'd relent only if Hanoi's leaders agreed to take steps to end the conflict. Johnson again threatened a bigger war. Hanoi did not blink. The Viet Cong was financially backed and well supplied by communist China and Soviet forces. Hanoi did not back down, and Johnson sent troops by the thousands and continued his air attacks.

Ψ

Early in March of 1968 senator McCarthy had a near victory in the New Hampshire presidential primary, winning 42 percent of the vote to Johnson's 50 percent. McCarthy's success was entirely unexpected, unprecedented and led Johnson to rethink his fallibility. In anticipation of the vice president's easy win of the Democratic nomination Johnson announced of the ending of the bombing over North Vietnam. On Thursday, October 31, four nights before the general election, Americans were given a treat—and then a trick from Dick. Senator George Smathers (D-FL) relayed the message to the president that "the word is out that we are making an effort to throw the election to Humphrey. Nixon has been told of it."[11]

The president liked to brag that he had Humphrey's "pecker in my pocket." The Texas-spun double entendre was plucked from an earlier statement Johnson made while discussing a political assistant. "I don't want loyalty. I want *loyalty.* I want him to kiss my ass in Macy's window at high noon and tell me it smells like roses. I want his pecker in my pocket."[12]

The deals made that summer ensured that whoever won the party's nomination could end the war in his own way. Both the president and Chicago's mayor—Richard Daley—anticipated demonstrators at the convention. The president was confident in mayor Daley's ability to control them.

Chapter Three

A Party Divided

Gans and Lowenstein had set out in 1967 to find an anti-war candidate to head the Democratic ticket. On September 23 they met with New York Senator Robert F. Kennedy. He declined to run. California congressman Don Edwards also declined, as did Idaho Senator Frank Church, Canadian-born economist John K. Galbraith, General James M. Gavin, and South Dakota Senator George S. McGovern. On October 20, after meeting with Lowenstein, Minnesota Senator Eugene McCarthy agreed to run for his party's nomination for president. At the end of November McCarthy officially declared his candidacy, citing his concern for an administration that had no apparent limit to the price it was willing to pay for military victory.

Continuing his plan to unseat an incumbent president, Lowenstein urged the YDFL Party to send sixteen of its members to Waverly, Minnesota. Vice President Hubert Humphrey had invited constituents to meet with him at his home in hopes of salvaging support for the president. Humphrey reminded the YDFL students of Johnson's 1964 Great Society programs. He reminded them of all the civil rights legislation Johnson had signed into law. Lowenstein and the students found little tolerance for the president's present actions despite the past. Sensing he was not going the win back any support for his boss, the vice president told Lowenstein his earlier letter-writing campaign had been a wasted effort (in 1966 students had sent letters to the president and other government officials urging them to shift their policies. The letters demanded decisive action should be taken to end the War in Vietnam). Lowenstein then suggested that if the letters were a wasted effort and they could not change the president's mind, perhaps they should change the president. Kaibel, a student body president from Minnesota, found the idea brilliantly radical, saying, "It was electrifying, portentous! The idea that an incumbent president of one's own party could or should be unseated is mind boggling!"[1]

Earlier that year while on a trip to California, Lowenstein observed students lying down in front of troop trains. He watched other defiant acts of disobedience to protest the war. Lowenstein told the protesters such tactics were the wrong approach and should only be a last resort, that it was imperative to make the political system work. Democracy should be given a chance. He advised that the student Democrats needed to present themselves to Johnson as a constituency, suggesting the administration would be more receptive to a coalition of the people it served rather than a rogue group of dissenters.

Kaibel gathered student body presidents, and together they drafted a letter to President Johnson. Lowenstein thought the tone of the first draft sounded too incensed and lacked persuasiveness. He said the letter had to convey that the potential constituents of the administration were responsible, judicious people. One hundred student body presidents finally agreed to a weaker, yet assertive, version of the letter. It was eventually printed in the *New York Times.* Via conference call, student body presidents from all over the country confirmed the letter's sentiments. The letter was signed by all the student presidents and sent to Washington, DC (this was the letter-writing campaign Humphrey had called a waste of time). Lowenstein urged student presidents to save all the articles they had regarding war protests. He collected the letters and used them to influence people to anonymously contribute to their cause.

The students went to face their constituents in person. Funds donated by the Ford Foundation made it possible for twenty-five student body presidents to fly to New York.[2] They met in a conference room at Kennedy airport with Johnson's national security advisor. McGeorge Bundy and other administration staff met with the students for what was supposed to be an open exchange of ideas on the draft and the war. Lowenstein had instructed the group's spokesman to press the issue on the war and get some sound answers from a politician. Kaibel was persistent and repeatedly questioned Bundy on why the president was not responding to a constituency that blatantly opposed the war. The security advisor was evasive, if not dismissive. The president had told him to "get those goddamned intellectuals to stop eating my ass!" Bundy obliged by telling the students, "You are not going to change the president, no matter what you do with this kind of stuff."[3]

Secretary of State Dean Rusk also consented to meet students. Kaibel intended to prove that the US could not support a coalition government in Vietnam. He whimsically sheathed his anger with an analogy of a fox and a chicken coop, asking Rusk why the "Communists always have the sly and wily foxes and we wind up with the dumb clucks."[4]

Kaibel had been a loyal Humphrey supporter since the Civil Rights Movement. A meeting was arranged with the vice president. At first Humphrey admonished Kaibel for his flippancy with secretary Rusk. He then explained how the Communists were criminals. Humphrey reminisced, recalling how they used to fight people in Minnesota when they tried to gain control of the DFL party. He implored Kaibel and his followers to go out and fight criminals who threaten to control things. Kaibel's man behind the curtain was a traitor who now kowtowed to Johnson's policies. The feisty Minnesota politician who, in 1948, had urged the Democratic Party to "get out of the shadows of states' rights and walk forthrightly into the bright sunshine of human rights" had changed. Kaibel left his meeting with the vice president disillusioned. He was saddened that any trace of the man he once knew was gone. Lowenstein consoled the younger Kaibel, telling him that deep down, in his heart, Humphrey was still the same liberal.

A coup had been orchestrated in Washington, DC. Lowenstein instructed representatives of the various student bodies to find leaders in their respective schools to help remove Johnson from office. Kaibel brought the idea to Maurice Visscher. He loved it and advised that Kaibel organize a committee whose goal was to move the dissenting DFL party members in a direction that discouraged Johnson from seeking another term. A planning committee, overseen by Forest Harris, was formed. Two of the people on that committee were Fred and Barbara Amram.

Chapter Four

A Coincidental Progression

Barbara Frances Flowerman was born in the Bronx, New York in January 1932. Her parents, Harry and Nettie Flowerman (née Wolf) were first-generation Americans who practiced a liberal, Reform Judaism. They were cultural Jews. During the Great Depression they always had money and food on the table. Harry was an optometrist with an office in the East Bronx. In high school Barbara was involved with liberal groups such as the Ethical Cultural Society. Harry brought home liberal newspapers such as *PM, The Star* and *The Daily Compass.* The left-wing papers were published in New York City from the mid-1940s to the early 1950s and greatly influenced Barbara, creating a sharp social conscience and an acute moral compass. On Sundays Harry listened to WQXR, a public radio station in New York that broadcast lectures from the Ethical Cultural Society.

In 1948 Barbara took a position as a counselor at Camp Solidarity in New Jersey. Always cognizant of the state of the world and its future, she intended to share her political buttons with others at the camp. In the general election that year she supported Progressive Party candidate Henry Wallace. Political solicitation was not allowed at the camp, and the Wallace buttons were never seen. She did, however, meet a fellow Wallace supporter—a camper named Fred Amram.

Manfred Amram was born to Meinhardt and Sitta Amram (née Nussbaum) September 1933 in Hannover, Germany. Adolf Hitler had been elected chancellor of Germany in January. Following a National Socialist Party rally in September 1935, anti-Jewish laws began to be enforced. With each new law, Jews lost another civil right. When Manfred was five, his mother took him to the park. He noticed that the benches were marked "nur für Juden" (only for Jews), and "nur für Arier" (Aryans). Initially the markings' true implications were not clear to him. Gradually the freedoms to do things like going to have ice cream at the local parlor, or ride the trolley with his mother, disappeared. In 1938, radios were taken from Jewish homes. In July a law was passed requiring Jews to carry identification cards. That winter, from the balcony of their fourth-floor apartment Manfred witnessed Kristallnacht (Night of Broken Glass). Shops owned by Jews were destroyed. Shards of glass filled the streets. Flames from synagogues poured into the night sky as Jews were beaten in the streets. They were humiliated, spat on, and forced to scrub streets with small brushes. Between November 9 and 10, in Germany and parts of Austria, ninety-one Jews were killed; thirty thousand were arrested and sent to concentration camps. Over one thousand synagogues were burned, and over seven thousand Jewish businesses were destroyed. After Kristallnacht, desecration of Jewish-owned businesses was common. "Aryanization" increased, and those businesses were transferred to Germans.

As a Jewish business owner, Meinhardt was pursued by the Gestapo. When they came to the door, demanding to see Meinhardt, Manfred or Sitta claimed he was not home. Amram hid in the lower levels of the five-story apartment building where they lived. Eventually the Geheime Staatspolizei (secret state police) caught Meinhardt and confiscated his automobile and the materials he used in his fabric business. He was arrested and put on a *Tiefbau* (a forced road construction crew). Laborers were given a choice of going home at night or sleeping in barracks on site. Meinhardt chose the former and was told that if he did not show up for work, his entire family would be killed. Sitta, much more than Meinhardt, knew they had to get out of Germany. She arranged for the services of the Hebrew Immigrant Aid Society (HIAS) to help them find a US sponsor. HIAS located a doctor who vouched for the Amrams. In October 1939 Meinhardt eluded the Tiefbau. He and his family made their way off the continent by way of Holland and Belgium. In the early morning of November 15 Manfred followed his father up on the deck of the *Pennland.* They watched as the Statue of Liberty dwarfed their ship. Upon arrival in America Meinhardt was Americanized to Milton, and Manfred became Fred. Sitta, refusing hysterically to be another Sarah (the uniform pejorative name for Jewish women in Nazi Germany), remained Sitta.

In the fall of 1948, from his family's 77th Street apartment on Manhattan's east side, Fred campaigned for Henry Wallace. When camp ended that summer he and Barbara agreed to stay in touch with each other. Flowerman also campaigned for Wallace and running mate Senator Glen Taylor (D-ID). She watched singer, activist and actor Paul Robeson perform at Madison Square Garden as a campaign event. She also attended a rally for Wallace that featured a performance by Woody Guthrie. A song suggested the two parties, Democrat and Republican, had more similarities than contradictions.

> "The donkey is tired and thin
> The elephant thinks he'll move in
> They yell and they fuss but they ain't foolin' us,
> 'cause they're brothers right under the skin.
> Which one will you ride this year?"

Chapter Five

The "Mystic"

Henry Agard Wallace began in politics supporting the Republican Party. He was among three Republicans that Roosevelt appointed to his cabinet. He was progressive, though, and had supported the Democratic presidential candidate, Alfred Smith, in 1928. Smith had been governor of New York and was known for progressive reforms. He was an anti-prohibition candidate and attracted a lot of drinkers. Smith's politics also appealed to the voters that were tired of the corruption, the speakeasies and bootlegging brought by prohibition.

Wallace came from Iowa and was most knowledgeable about agriculture. Historian Arthur M. Schlesinger, Jr. described Wallace as the best Secretary of Agriculture the country has ever had; he served in that position from 1933 to 1940. When he was chosen as Roosevelt's running mate, conservative Democrats were skeptical. Wallace was an old-school liberal reformer and New Dealer. He was seen as a "renegade Republican," or "mystic apostle." To many he represented all that was objectionable in the manipulative, bureaucracy-bound New Deal.

The 1940 Democratic National Convention began with "boos" resonating through Chicago Stadium. When Roosevelt's selection of Wallace was announced, delegates were moved to rebellion. The president displayed his loyalty to his choice, threatening to decline his own nomination if Wallace was not accepted. Eleanor delivered a speech to conciliate the protesting party members. Her words assuaged opposition of Wallace, and with a 449 to 82 Electoral College vote, he became the nation's 33rd vice president.

Wallace disagreed with many of the president's policies, and by 1942 Roosevelt was often at odds with him, particularly with regard to the Soviet Union. Wallace was too far left and closely aligned with labor for many of the president's advisors. In a Gallup poll taken before the Democratic Party's 1944 vice presidential nomination, 65 percent favored Wallace's reelection. Truman polled at 2 percent.

Henry Wallace was thought to be eccentric. The president's health was also an issue. His advisors questioned Wallace's ability to succeed him if he did not survive a fourth term. Harry S. Truman (D-MO) was also being considered as a running mate. At the 1944 Democratic National Convention Wallace had a sizable lead over the other candidates. However, he lacked the majority necessary to secure the nomination. He began to win votes and was on his way to winning the nomination. Fate interceded, and officials were tricked into shutting the Chicago Stadium down for a day. Mayor Edward Joseph Kelly and officials, including Associate US Supreme Court Justice James F. Byrnes, strongly opposed Wallace's nomination. The convention's postponement resulted in Truman getting a 2 percent bounce. Party leaders desperately tried to persuade delegates to vote for Truman. Various back-room deals were made. Postmaster positions and ambassadorships were offered in exchange for votes against Wallace. The shift in the second ballot tallies reflect this:

Candidate	Ballot 1	Ballot 2 (before shift)	Ballot 2 (after shift)
Henry Wallace (IA)	429.5	473	105
Harry Truman (MO)	319.5	477.5	1,031
John Bankhead (AL)	98	23.50	0

In what was dubbed the "second Missouri Compromise"[1] Truman won the nomination for vice president. The Roosevelt-Truman ticket achieved a 432-99 electoral vote in the election, defeating the Republican ticket of Thomas Dewey and John Bricker. Harry Truman was sworn in as vice president on January 20, 1945.

Franklin Delano Roosevelt passed away April 12, 1945. That afternoon, Eleanor called Truman to inform him her husband had died of a massive cerebral hemorrhage. The vice president's first concern was for Mrs. Roosevelt, and he asked if there was anything he could do. She replied, "Is there anything we can do for you? You are the one in trouble now."[2] Later that day, Truman was sworn in as president. Henry Wallace had missed the chance to be the 33rd President of the United States by eighty-two days.

In 1948 the Progressive Party reinvented itself (an attempt to have a third party had failed in 1920). At the Democratic National Convention in Philadelphia, incumbent Harry Truman initially put in place a plank in his party's platform for Civil Rights. Minneapolis Mayor Hubert Humphrey proposed a plank named after Andrew Biemiller (US Representative for Wisconsin's fifth district). Humphrey and Biemiller worked together to establish a strong civil rights plank. In his speech at the convention, Humphrey laid the groundwork for future Democrats. His shrill timbered voice wrapped around a clarion call that shot through the convention center:

"The time has arrived in America for the Democratic Party to get out of the shadows of states' rights and walk forthrightly into the bright sunshine of human rights...!"[3]

Truman knew that any platform based on civil rights was likely to cause Southern delegates to walk out in protest. Ignorant of the losses to himself, the former hat salesman maintained that civil rights were an important moral issue. The radical plank passed by sixty-nine votes. It was supported by many urban party leaders who thought doing so secured them the black vote for future elections. It passed 651.5 to 582.5, causing Strom Thurmond and a dozen Southern delegates to walk out of the hall.[4] Thurmond bolted the party and ran that year for president as candidate of the State's Rights Democratic Party (colorfully known as the Dixiecrats).

Ψ

Fred Amram was attending Syracuse University in 1951. Barbara Flowerman had been studying anthropology and sociology at Queens College, graduating in the spring of 1953 with a Bachelor of Arts degree in social work. The following fall she went to the University of Chicago for graduate school. After graduating in 1955 with a master's degree, she returned to New York where she began work at the New York State Psychiatric Institute.

Fred graduated from Syracuse University with a Bachelor of Science degree in Speech Education in January of 1956. He was impressed by Barbara's knowledge and interest in the world. They had kept in contact through letters and phone calls—with varied frequency—since their meeting at Camp Solidarity in 1948. When Barbara returned to New York in 1955 they reunited, and on February 5, 1956 they were married.

A communications professor at Syracuse recommended the University of Minnesota's graduate program to Amram. He and Barbara left for Minnesota in the fall of 1956. They found a small apartment at 1929 Fremont Avenue in Minneapolis, four blocks from Lake of the Isles. Fred was first employed as a graduate teaching assistant at the University. He rose through the ranks—instructor, assistant professor, associate professor—eventually becoming a professor. Barbara was working as a social worker at the Washburn Child Guidance Clinic.

After two years in a small apartment they began looking for a house. Barbara's salary was significantly higher than Fred's, but when they applied for a loan, the bank did not take her income into consideration because she was a woman. Homes in Minneapolis, especially those near the lakes, were desirable to the couple, but based only on Fred's income, they were not eligible for a loan large enough to buy a Minneapolis home. They were finally able to get a smaller loan from a credit union. Richfield, a suburb bordering Minneapolis, was suggested to them. In May 1959, they purchased a 1,100 square-foot rambler at 7337 Aldrich Avenue South for $14,000.

The segregation, degradation and human injustice Fred Amram had witnessed in Germany sensitized him. The experiences of Kristallnacht and seeing his father forced to work by the Nazis made him more aware of the suppression of a minority. He was, as a result, hyper-sensitive to social injustices and opportunities for civil rights to advance in a democracy. Henry Wallace and a mutual interest in world and local politics were important factors in bringing Barbara Flowerman and Fred Amram together. Because of what they had read, listened to or witnessed in their childhoods, each was inclined to take a stand when others did not. Both had an extraordinarily receptive moral compass and saw a need to put an immediate stop to violations of human rights. The timing was right. Fred and Barbara came to Minnesota in the year that the embers of the First Indochina War were being fanned to grow into the inferno that was the Second Indochina War—the Vietnam War.

Ψ

Early in 1953, President Eisenhower was urged by the French to send aid to the fighting in French-Indochina. The conflict, known as the

First Indochina War, pitted the French against Chinese communists. The president sent Lieutenant General John "Iron Mike" O' Daniel to Vietnam to assess the situation. Eisenhower's chief of staff, Matthew Ridgway, advised against US involvement. Despite his foresight that "this war would absorb our troops by division,"[5] Eisenhower sent bombers and non-combat personnel to the French. Still they fought a losing battle, and the president sent additional aid that included aircraft equipped with napalm for clearing foliage.

The French fort in Dien Bien Phu, a city in northwestern Vietnam, fell to the Communists in May of 1954. Eisenhower's reaction to the French defeat was to form an alliance to defend Vietnam from Communism. The Southeast Asia Treaty Organization (SEATO) was signed in September 1954, aligning us with the United Kingdom, France, New Zealand and Australia. The pact stipulated that the US participate in conflicts as an observer only. The treaty was signed, and France and the Chinese Communists agreed to divide Vietnam at the seventeenth parallel. Historians argue that by not taking an active part in the Geneva peace agreement between the French and the Communists, Eisenhower had kept the US out of Vietnam conflict. However, by forming SEATO, he inadvertently left the US subject to being pulled into the growing conflict.

The US sent support to assist Ngô Đình Diêm[7] in subverting Communism. General J. Lawton Collins was sent as an ambassador to what was called "Free Vietnam" (the term South Vietnam was not used until 1955). Collins was instructed to assist Diêm in building an army to mobilize and wage a military campaign. In February 1955, US soldiers were sent to Vietnam to act as military advisors. They were instructed to oversee the formation of Diêm's army. Eventually South Vietnam was declared, by President Diêm, to be the Republic of Vietnam (RVN).

In October, Eisenhower formally recognized the new republic. His first action was to offer military, economic and technical assistance. By 1960 Eisenhower had increased the number of military advisors in South Vietnam to nine hundred. As he left the White House to the new Kennedy administration, his advice was to make the containment of Communism a priority. He told Kennedy he considered the small country of Laos, on Vietnam's western edge, to be "the cork in the bottle."[6]

Chapter Six

The Progressive Gene

One could say I was conceived during a news segment in the winter of 1964. As the Amrams watched the piece produced by Minnesota television journalist Dave Moore, the idea of adopting was reinforced. It was about babies of different races and ethnicity that were waiting to be adopted. After the birth of their first child in 1962, the couple chose to adopt. Moore's piece influenced them to adopt a child of mixed race, although they were impartial as to which races. On February 23, 1965, the couple came with their two-year old daughter to the Children's Home Society in St. Paul. There I was, busting to begin some kind of life. The Amrams and their daughter offered an interesting, educational and exciting one.

The interracial couple who created me existed independently, somewhere. As an adult, I learned of my mother and formed a relationship with her. My biological father, however, chose to maintain his distance. Fred is the only father I'll ever know personally. My mother, Barbara, tells a somewhat disturbing story. When I was two years old she was carrying me through a Walgreens store. A black man—much darker than myself—walked by us. I asked, "Why is that man's skin ishy?" I can't imagine her embarrassment. At age two the apple fell quite far from the tree.

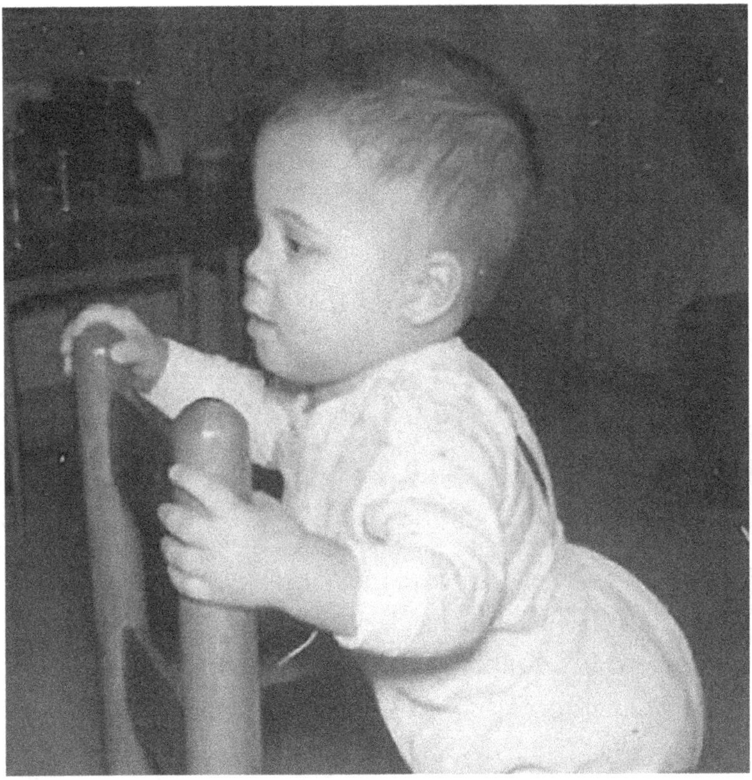

Me in 1966

My dab of brown in the neighborhood nudged the status-quo. When DFL members and neighbors came to the house and found me in my playpen, it indicated that Fred and Barbara were progressive. I had a ringside seat at a pivotal time in America and a mother who saw the realities in life. She showed America where they were and where they needed to go to be ready for the future. In later years, the idea that "Black is beautiful" sublimated my mind. The sentiment was expressed on buttons, bumper-stickers and in poems during the early 1970s. To me it meant biracial must be at least half as beautiful and intriguing. Indomitable afros in which a comb could last throughout the day were in vogue. In the mid-'60s though, before the media decided we were beautiful, a white couple adopting a baby of mixed race was newsworthy. When I was three or four, reporters for the *Minneapolis Star* interviewed my parents on biracial adoption.

Mom, Susan and me in 1968.
Photo courtesy of the *Richfield Sun*

Our home was exceedingly liberal and did not match the notion that a woman's place was anywhere in particular. If I went to a friend's house to show off my latest Hot Wheels cars, the chances were that his mother was in the kitchen cooking something. Or if I knocked on the door, I'd hear the noise of vacuum cleaner abruptly stop. A woman with a kerchief tied on her her head usually opened it hastily, and I saw dust filtering through the sunlight. I went in and smelled a lingering lemon scent. However, if a friend knocked on our door, the odds were that my mother was on the phone calling on behalf of Senator McCarthy. Boxes of literature were open in corners, and the smell of newsprint hinted in the room. It sublimated their young mind, raising the hope that the kid went home to tell his parents to vote for Gene. That's just how it was, how my mom was. It's how my friend's moms were… different, for the most part, in what they did. Few of the moms on our block had exactly the same values as my mom. Or maybe they did, but just chose not to act like she did. Their priorities were different. That's how I remember it.

Well-trimmed lawns lined our street. It was residential, and roars and hums of mowers, proximal and distant, raced to beat the daylight. We used to yell to each other and savor the grass scent when it was cut. Our operations soldiered on as crows *cawwed* murderously. They protected us, though, flying against a hazed sallow sky from one end of the block to the other like sentries. Each day provided optimism and anticipation for the next. There were always friends out in the evenings, and we all promised to meet up somewhere again after dinner. They were verbal agreements. We had no methods for text. We needed to communicate in order to play. During the day, we pushed Tonka trucks or crawled behind dump trucks. We dragged road graders through sandboxes and graded the roads that went through our neighbors' yards. If we were bored, feeling creative, destructive or vindictive, we held magnifying glasses toward the sun at high noon. Our toy soldiers melted in an agonizingly slow death. The green plastic figures were recognized as the enemy and we watched them ooze to tiny puddles in the dirt. If we wanted to taste the earth we dared each other to eat common things that crawled on the ground.

We invented games, some with an element of danger. On fall evenings, after our chores were complete, kids rolled inside barrels of leaf sweepers. The sun started to slip behind the maple trees. We ignored it and clung together. Séances convened randomly in yards, and we bowed to nature, conceding the day's end while ensuring another. We worshiped the echoes of our summers, trying to stretch the evenings out until school began again. Sometimes the older girl across the street entertained us. We took turns spinning from her tanned arms like helicopter blades. Her silky brown hair smell mixed with the mown grass scent. We studied her bare feet for the blades poking between her toes.

Our house stood midway in the block. It was a white rambler with aluminum awnings over the front windows and door. It had brown trim, and a brown-washed picket fence my dad built circled the backyard. In the fall, a crab apple tree littered the backyard with its fruit. My sister and I found work as the less migrant type of workers. We were paid ten cents a bucket. Eventually my dad hired a neighbor kid who negotiated a higher wage. Our front doorbell clunked with a reserved sound. It was almost inaudible from the outside. Inside it wasn't much louder. Its unpretentious clunk was just loud enough to let you know a guest waited patiently under the awning. Configured between two similar sized ramblers, ours stood out with one affectation. The mezuzah[1] on our door frame was angled perfectly. It let visitors know they were calling on a family that observed the Sabbath on Saturday. The Jewish adornment suggested the Amrams might be inclined to take a stand for minority groups. It hinted that they might even be bothered to get involved and better society.

Aldrich house as it looks today

Consciously or unconsciously, kids notice change in visual and audible stimuli. Toward the end of 1967 the level of activity in our house changed. The times I saw my mom on the phone or stuffing envelopes increased. Voices raised in pitch. Many DFL meetings and committees filled my parents' evenings. My sister and I grew to expect their absence at least once a week. Babysitters clunked at the door more frequently. The older girl across the street sat with us sometimes. Donna, our neighbor across the street, had a daughter who sat with us more often. She was the oldest of three and went to Richfield's Catholic high school, The Academy of the Holy Angels. She was strict and not likely to bend the rules. I preferred the girl who spun my friends and me on summer nights. She was the youngest of four and went to Richfield High School. Carol was more likely to bend the rules. Every time she sat with us I asked her to read to me from "Johnny Wonder" in the comic section of the *Minneapolis Star* and do the puzzles.

Lilac hedges grew in one corner of our backyard. They blossomed early each spring and scented the air, drifting lavender petals to the front walk that I danced around in hopscotches. I woke up mornings in the summers of 1968 to 1970 to the sounds of birds screeching their songs. I was adroit. I thought I was invincible, and the neighborhood world was my own. I was inquisitive and probably had a little better idea than any of my friends of what was going on in the world. Those were the first summers I remember. Fate suggested that it would be my first childhood.

Sunshine pounded our sidewalk to an opaque pulpit. I pontificated to myself on the premeditated merits of my day. The metal awning over the front door shadowed rows of ant hills caught between the cracks in the walk. I ran out and thought nothing of trampling over the hills, scattering the homes of ants. In 1969 I was given a blue and white bike. I mounted it and promptly rode away. My regimen began with rousting my friends to patrol our neighborhood. The first check-point was usually a Gulf Gas station on 75th in Lyndale. The giant blue "Gulf" in an orange circle always looked like it aspired to something. We bought baseball cards and looked if there were any new ones. The thin sticks of gum that came with the cards always fell apart in my mouth. Wooden clothespins held the cards in our bike spokes. A steep hill dividing 73rd street from Oak Grove Boulevard was a daring coast. In the winter we trespassed frequently, entering a fenced yard at the top of the hill with flexible fliers, saucers or toboggans. Or, for a less spurious slide, sometimes my mom took my sister and me to a big hill in Augsburg Park. Afterward, she usually found us something to read at the library.

Me, sis and some friends

By the early 1970s my staple Saturday morning cartoon evolution had become infused with liberal paces of *In the News* and *Schoolhouse Rock*. I was entertained and educated. *Schoolhouse*

Rock, among other things, taught about civics. Catchy songs and animated images told how a bill became a law, or taught about the power of the veto or filibuster. *In the News* was concise. It began, as I recall, with planet earth spinning like a giant blue marble. The two-minute bits were kid-friendly. They appealed to a kid's sense of wonder. The segments were about positive, constructive things going on in developing nations.

And on those evenings of séance, as the sun sank to mesh what lies beyond bucolic gerrymanders, neighbors' TVs flickered through windows into the night. We glanced up occasionally from our operations to see the codes. The intermittent glares reflected on windows told my friends when to go home. Their parents were watching Cronkite deliver the CBS nightly news report. The "most trusted man in America" delivered casualty numbers to the parents who sheltered their kids from the war. They were the parents of many of my peers who were ostensibly indifferent to the war's endurance. They did not see the bleak possibility that, under the current administration, the conflict in Southeast Asia could last long enough to draft their sons. I went home when the crickets commenced, and the stingray bikes clicked gently in the night.

I entered my home as strained voices whispered behind me. My dad sat talking with our next door neighbor on his step. They smoked cigarettes and sipped at cans of Hamm's or Grain Belt beer. Our next-door neighbor, Dave, was a high-voltage tester for Northern States Power. They chatted about sports and laughed about the neighborhood gossip. Their laughs, especially Dave's, rolled deep into the evening. As the conversation lagged and quiet enraptured the block, their whispers suggested the lady who lived across the street was bigoted and rumored to spy from her window. The allegation, from 1966, hinted that she had looked through binoculars to locate my crib. Rumors went around the neighborhood, though, that she still looked into our house from across the street. Her curtain fell as my dad and Dave talked.

They paused for her shadow to pass. Talk began again, and their whispers lulled the twilight.

My biological mother was not Jewish, and according to Orthodox law, my chances of being recognized as a genuinely righteous Jew were limited. Befittingly, the Amrams were Reform in their practice. Incidentally, the irony was that a few neighbors said I looked like my mom because we both had black curly hair and blue eyes (a gift from my biological mother). One day, soon after the Amrams brought me home in 1965, the woman across the street clunked at our door, waiting nervously under the awning.

"Oh—what a lovely baby!" she said with slight hesitation.

She spoke of a baby as any mother might. To her, I'm sure I was a "lovely baby," but I was also a tinge darker than most on the block. For that, I suspect I earned a special classification in her mind. Variations of the story have been told through the years. One even suggested that, after seeing me, the neighbors threatened to put their houses on the market.[1]

Initially three-fourths of my grandparents had negative opinions concerning my adoption. Archival testimonies confirm that both of my mom's parents voiced opposition. Only my dad's mother had an issue with it though. I called her Oma, a familiar form of the German word for grandma. Oma had a prejudiced side. This manifested itself, most notably to me, by her disparagement of her sister-in-law for selecting a Polish Jew as her second husband. There was a defined elitist quality about Oma. In spite of the oppression she witnessed, or the subjugation in which she was nearly included, I'm told that deep in her soul she was a bigot. In Hannover, prior to a 1935 Nuremburg Law restricting the employment of German females under forty-five in Jewish households, she had enjoyed the services of a maid. When they settled in New York's Washington Heights in 1939, Sitta had to work making paper flowers. She hated it. Milton I knew as Opa, a German form of grandpa. He died when I was three years old. All that I've been told of him indicates that he was quiet and easy-going, apparently free of prejudice. Fred and Barbara adopted me regardless of the animosity it might bring between them and their parents. I love that insolent defiance—especially when bigotry is the victim.

We visited my mom's parents once or twice a year at Century Village. It was a gated retirement community in West Palm Beach, Florida. Its population was predominantly white, and they employed a sentry to stand in a little booth who inspected the contents of cars. The village was quite explicit regarding its policies on children and sternly discouraged them or banned them from places such as the village's clubhouse. Complexes of villas were arranged, sequentially, by numbers. Letters designated the individual villas. Pristine white sidewalks edged immaculately trimmed hedges. The hum of a weary air conditioner was the vacant sound of the village's sedentary world. At the end of the walk bristly grass poked its wide, pointed blades.

One other incident, possibly racially motivated, sticks in my mind. Like their apartment in New York, my grandmother kept the villa in a perpetual state of austerity. An air-tight seal sedated you as you entered the unit. To the left of the door two recliners flanked a small table. I always chose one of these as my chair of choice on our visit. My grandfather always looked disturbed and uncomfortable when I jumped in, pushed my feet out and put my head back. I wore my hair long, often unkempt, in the early 70s. I hated haircuts.

"Michael, do you have to put your head back so hard?" he asked.

I took his request in a racist way. Was something wrong with my head—or my hair for that matter—touching his precious doilies? To be fair, Harry Flowerman wasn't wild about *anyone* laying on the sofa in their villa, or flagrantly treating the place like it was their own. Still, I felt singled out. Mostly, though, I was just a brash kid who didn't like being told what I couldn't do.

Harry let down his doilies—and his teeth—for me. I endeared myself to him in my own way. In the winter of 1969 he and Nettie took my mom, Susan and me on a Caribbean cruise. One night, after dinner, grandpa was brushing his teeth, and I noticed the big off-pink gums toying with my young instincts for mischief from their little green dish. The next day I ran up and down the winterized pool deck of the *SS France* publicizing the 'toy teeth.' My only grampa was a sport. I ingratiated myself to him.

Oma never said a racist word to me. I can't remember her ever asking that I not do something. She always indulged my sister and me in her pristine apartment in north Miami. Sometimes she even played with us on the floor. Oma never lost her German accent and, in her later years, sometimes had to 'fish' for English words. German Jews are not known for their use of Yiddish. The language—first known to be used in the twelfth century AD—was spoken by Jews as a means of communication in the ghettos of Eastern Europe. Some German Jews feel the language denotes a lesser class. When his family arrived in New York in 1939 Opa used the language to converse with people helping them. Growing up, though, I can't recall Oma or my dad ever speaking Yiddish. It was generally considered to be a language of boorish people and Poles. Conversely, my mom was of Eastern European Jewish descent. Yiddish is an interesting and colorful language. She often used words and phrases to make a point or teach as a different way of looking at a situation. Her lessons might begin with, "As my mother used to say." Or, if something had an unrealistic or highly unlikely premise, she said, "And if grandma had wheels she'd be a trolley car." (The phrase translates to a Yiddish expression). If our whole family got together—my mom's sister's family—she said it was the *ganze mischpache*, literally the whole family.

Chapter Seven

Assassinations of Character

My sister was delivered on election day in 1962. On Tuesday, November 6 there were few local races. Not too much was at stake in Richfield. The mid-term election elected members to the 88th United States Congress. Republicans gained four seats in the House of Representatives and Democrats maintained a majority in both houses of congress. Despite his New Frontier program's failure to pass, Kennedy remained victorious. Everything looked good for 1963—until November.

On a Friday afternoon, Kennedy's motorcade, in an unscheduled routing, wound through Dealey Plaza in Dallas. My mom was tending to her one-year-old daughter in the kitchen. Most likely the radio was tuned to MPR (Minnesota public radio) or WCCO. Her happiness as a new mother turned to shock and concern for the future. She was likely concerned for the future of her child.

Democrats and Republicans felt an overwhelming sense of despair. The man who had promised to land a man on the moon by the decade's end was gone. All the hope Kennedy had inspired for a peaceful future was lost with one—or two—bullets. Within hours of the assassination, Vice President Lyndon Baines Johnson was sworn in as our thirty-sixth president. He took the oath of office aboard Air Force One as it taxied on Dallas's Love Field. He placed his hand on a Catholic missal[1] found on Kennedy's desk inside the plane, and federal Judge Sarah T. Hughes, the first woman to do so, administered the oath.

Ψ

In addition to teaching communication and creativity, my dad was assistant director of the HELP (Higher Education for Low-income Parents) Center at the University of Minnesota. Founded in 1967, the program initially was designed to assist single mothers or fathers, including helping them find appropriate employment. The single parents received training as well as education. They worked toward certificates and degrees, receiving the tutoring or counseling they needed. The program also provided advocacy so the parents could attain support from the welfare department. The welfare assistance facilitated child care which gave the parents time to go to school.

By 1969 the HELP Center's goals—and acronym—had changed. The P now stood for people. Its services were expanded to include minority groups. Its recipients included African-Americans, Hispanics and Native Americans. Convicts were counseled, trained and given skills to rehabilitate themselves. If they were in prison, or had been to prison, their potential for college was assessed. If they were found to be candidates for the HELP program, they were included as low-income people. My dad made sure that adequate funding was available, adequate faculty was employed and that necessary space was located. Forrest Harris, professor of social and behavioral science in the University's General College, was director of the HELP Center. Harris, in his capacity as DFL vice chairman, acquainted my dad with top people in the party, among them US Senator Walter Mondale and Vice President Hubert Humphrey.

In 1972 Harris resigned his position as director at the HELP Center. He went on to head the social studies division in the General

College, but still advised my dad in the role of director. One of the director's jobs was to secure federal funds for the program. Annually my dad traveled to Washington, DC. In front of a senate subcommittee he laid out his case for proper funding of the U of M HELP Center program. Johnson's War on Poverty had left sizable monies available for social causes. However, numerous liberal programs vied for funding, and its assets were quickly exhausted. If money for the HELP program was not available at the federal level, my dad went to the county or city coffers. Hennepin and Ramsey counties had sparse funds. Senator Mondale coached my dad on what to say to the committees at the federal level, and he also arranged for him to meet with county commissioners at the state level.

The assassination of Martin Luther King caused riots in Minneapolis. One positive effect of the unrest was that they pulled minorities from the corners of society. The Johnson administration's Great Society programs had placed a strong emphasis on building families. Walter Mondale was chairman of a Senate subcommittee on children and youth. He authored legislation designed to improve the futures of families and children. Conservative groups opposed the interference of government into the family, resulting in Nixon's veto of most of Mondale's bills. Another argument against Mondale's proposals was that a working woman could potentially compromise the authority within the family. The young women in the HELP program were able to gain employment and make a better life for their children.

Faculty played a domino game to pass free time at the HELP center. The version of the game was learned from the inmates counseled at the state prison in Stillwater, Minnesota. The games took place at large tables in an abandoned church. There was my dad, Lou Bellamy, Joe Valentinetti and Ronnie Cousin. Bellamy was on the faculty in the General College. He stood 6'4" with a big afro and had a loud gummy laugh. My dad encouraged him to complete his Masters of Arts in theater. He did and eventually taught the subject. Joe Valentinetti was a counselor. He was a beatnik-type from New York City. He walked in lethargy and indifference and went whichever way the wind pointed his sandaled feet. His big shock of brown hair was disheveled, and he didn't care. He was said to write poetry and read Lawrence Ferlinghetti. Ronnie Cousin was another counselor at the HELP Center. I never knew Ronnie as well as the others.

In 1967 the HELP Center was housed in a very small space, and my dad secured a larger area for the program to expand. The center occupied an abandoned Episcopal church. My dad's office was in the church's basement in a room where the priest had slept, and Bellamy's office was in the kitchen. The area was small, and the smoke produced by a cigarette had few outlets. Occasionally my dad brought my sister and me to work with him. Sometimes it felt like I had been given clearance to be included in a clandestine scheme, and all the scratches on the steno pads were linked to spots that configured the war-sustaining domino theories. It was a covert operation to circumvent the Nixon vetoes and secure funding for the HELP center. The room they played in was tarry and black. Cigarette butts were snuffed in oddly shaped ash trays. In the early 70s my dad briefly smoked Benson & Hedges cigarettes. Plumes of smoke inundated the room, and figures of dominoes swam in them. The ivory dominoes made a smacking sound as they hit the wood. It echoed their having been "laid and played." A domino laid down and released was played. It could not be retracted. Random arrangements of the spotted "bones" formed a maze. Their ivory took on a yellow film, like the tusks of ancient elephants. Patterns of dominoes changed rapidly as the tiles were slapped on large wooden tables. *Hands* elapsed and bone concealing palms rhapsodized the rhythm of Cousin's gum chewing. Ivory bones were slid cunningly onto recreational grids until someone reached a score of 150.

For all I knew she was your average beautiful blonde-haired girl. It turned out that Melissa had a quarter Native American in her genes—enough to qualify her to be enrolled in a tribe. Her mother was single and initially had received an education from the HELP Center. Like us, Melissa visited with her parent. Occasionally our visits were in sync. Her hair was silky and bounced as she ran. It glistened under the hot choir room lights. The three of us invented games to play. We slid between stacked chairs and grand pianos. One day a game involved tossing a chalkboard eraser. I threw it up, and it landed on a rafter of lights. I never told anyone, and for years I feared I'd be implicated for arson. I'd be sentenced, serve twenty years at Stillwater State Prison, and be released as an accomplished domino player!

I'd be six-years-old in February, so I started in kindergarten the fall of 1970. My mom went back to work part-time at the U of M's Psychological Education Center. I walked with friends to the bus stop at the corner of our block. After writing my name and coloring for a half day, I went home on a bus. Usually I made it home in time for *Lunch with Casey.* The fictional engineer began his show by running from his train into the bunkhouse. Jones and Roundhouse Rodney had little skits featuring characters like Grandma Lumpet. Savoir-faire (a cartoon mouse) was everywhere as things we learned in school were affirmed by *Underdog* and *Klondike Cat.* On *Tennessee Tuxedo,* Phineas J. Whoopie routinely got his 3D-BB (three-dimensional blackboard) from the top shelf of an over-packed closet. He solved problems brought to him by a penguin and a walrus. Progress made toward the accurate portrayal of the Native American was lost as the US cavalry pursued two *Gopher Gulch Indians*. I watched through lunch and some days stayed to watch some of *Mel's* (Jass) *Matinee.* If I came home from school and my mom was not home from work, I went across the street to our neighbor. Donna was always welcoming; chewing gum, always with a cigarette lit somewhere. Her house smelled of smoke, and butts with lipstick marks peeked from ashtrays. I joined her son, Paul, on a big raggedy couch. We watched *Gomer Pyle* until my mom got home.

Holiday seasons came and opportunities for the teaching of cultural diversity usually followed. The faculty of the Richfield public schools always looked in a quandary over what they could do for, or with, the two or three Jewish kids. Chanukah—a minor Jewish Holiday—usually precedes Christmas on the Gregorian calendar by an adequate number of days to make a distinction between the two. Tuesday, December 22, we gathered at the menorah at 4:35 p.m. For the next seven nights we lit candles. We said the blessings, sang Maoz tzur and opened presents.

Chanukah fit nicely into the Richfield school's Christmas package that year. A feeling of isolation and defenselessness loomed over me at holiday time. It was a feeling of being singled out, a feeling feebly remedied by patronizing songs about clay dreidels. I don't know about my sister or the other three Jews, but I always resented the school's assumption that we'd ignore their insensitivity. I resented being expected to sing—or stand like an idiot while others sang—songs in music class about Mary and Jesus. Overtly religious songs, décor, or sentiments simply do not belong in a public school. That is what I was raised to believe. At age five I knew there was a lot not kosher about this idea. It was as though the Jeffersonian concept of separation of church and state had never entered the minds of some of the Richfield faculty. My mom saw an opportunity to teach the Richfield schools that others may hold different beliefs. What a concept in a melting pot. Meshuge (crazy). She had a keen sense of when the line dividing church and state was being blurred. I think everyone came to know the Amrams as agitators in Richfield. Someone had to do it, and I enjoyed being along for the ride, shaking windows and rattling walls as times were crying out for the change.

Ψ

Snowfall was sparse. It was Friday. The dusked hours of January 8, 1971 were crisp. To a kid, twenty-one degrees is inconsequential. A young driver was distracted by his friends in the back of his car. I was invincible in my neighborhood world of Hot Wheels and road graders. I was oblivious as five–year–old kids often are and pushed a lime green Tonka dump truck in his path. He was sober but only seventeen. Our next-door neighbor's son was the only witness. He was standing in the yard of the house of the binoculars woman, and called to me to come across the street. I heard the screech of a car's brakes and... BANG! I was struck by the grille of the car. Blood trickled from my right ear. My second childhood was due to begin in six weeks. Part of me was dislocated.

I arrived by ambulance at the intensive care unit of Fairview Southdale Hospital in Edina. Medical records state that Dr. Chisholm, head of pediatrics, who "happened to be upstairs in the pediatric ward," attended to me. An array of doctors took care of me, each specializing in a different area. In a consultation, R. Backus, M.D. reported, "Michael has had a rather serious cranial, cerebral trauma and the prognosis is probably poor but still guarded at this point..."[1] He gave my parents hope with medical jargon and, in doing so had left his options open. I was comatose and remained so for six weeks. Dr. Chisholm instructed my mom to pray.

"I am not very good at that," she replied.

Dr. Chisholm told my mom that he couldn't do his job if people did not pray. He was spiritual, and my mom was not. Credible doctors don't play God. They are merely educated navigators of fate who just try to tap into whatever their patient's loved one's belief system is. They state the facts, apply what science has taught them and let nature take its course. Prognoses are based on what the human body is capable of, and in my case I wager age was a factor. If I had been in my thirties, I expect that the prognosis would have left less of a margin for full recovery. I doubt my mom ever prayed. If she did send out an arbitrary prayer during those six weeks, I'll never know. The doctor will certainly never know. Only a convent of nuns might have known. Collectively, the sisters had their share of prescience. Knowledge of my coma channeled its way north through a divine pipeline (my dad had taught a creativity workshop at Saint Scholastica in Duluth—although I am told it preceded my coma).

The siren was silent. On Monday, February 1 the shadow of an ambulance eclipsed wisps of dead grass on highway wayside rests. I was stable, staring at the roof of an emergency vehicle, perhaps counting the infrequent minutes until childhood number two began. The coma was entering its fourth week. Nystagmus caused my eyes to flicker like those TV lights had on windows in neighbors' yards. Their pupils shifted in dizzying horizontals. The condition began immediately after the car hit me and remains to this day. I was being transferred to Mount Sinai Hospital in Minneapolis. The day also happened to be my sixth birthday. The move, though, was made because Fairview Southdale Hospital was not in Group Health's (my dad's insurance provider) network.

People do things that struggle to reach someone, even if the brain refuses to feel, see, hear, smell or taste them. Yvonne Ford knew me from my mom's work in the WILPF. She knew I watched *Lunch with Casey* (Jones) routinely, and she made a cake in the shape of a train engine.

"I cut pieces and stuck them together with chocolate frosting to make the engine."[2]

I've heard that random noises stimulate the comatose, so the TV in my hospital room was tuned to the show I had watched every day after writing my name in crayon for four hours. A tube inserted in my nose carried a nutritious milky liquid. I was not supposed to eat solid food, so my mom put some frosting on her finger and touched it to my mouth. Yvonne tied balloons to the bed, and the nurses sang to me. She knew someone who knew Roger Awsumb, the man behind Jones's red bandanna and called WTCN (channel 11). I don't think Casey or Roger ever physically appeared in my hospital room, but Roundhouse Rodney, Jones's sidekick, gave me an on-air birthday greeting.

Many people did things out of love, only to be appreciated by me months, even decades, later. Marie, the woman who had run the nursery school near the DFL headquarters in 1968, was among those who read to me. Donna compiled a photo album called "A Pocketful of Friends." It was a small rectangular turquoise album containing all my friends and babysitters on Aldrich Avenue.

I was discharged from Mount Sinai Hospital on March 11, 1971. The nurses were warm and loving. They all had bedside manners that spoiled me. I was later told they were quite taken with me and/or my hair. I left Sinai with some medicinal tablets and a reclining wheelchair. Its seat was covered with a fluffy imitation sheepskin, the kind one gets when they graduate from a hospital stay.

Back from the hospital world, I expected things to be just the same—in due time. I figured that, after strengthening my legs a bit, I could ride away on my bike just as I had that summer of 1969. *Anything was possible with the right amount of effort*, I thought. Stubbornness marinates in an unconscious mind. It stagnates and grows strong. My parents knew I needed to take a fall to know where I now stood. So out to the garage we went, if for nothing else, just to visit my blue and white bike. It was there, along with my hockey skates, just as I had left it thirty-five days ago. They took me from my wheelchair and set me on the bike. I was let down easily, and my job was clear—I had to accept that there were a few things I'd never do again.

For weeks the chair and I were inseparable, and reclining was my only recourse. When I was tilted upright, I fell forward like a jack-in-the-box clown. I felt lazy and useless. It was frustrating not being able to do simple tasks like tying my shoes or other personal needs a toilet-trained child takes for granted. However, what I found most frustrating was not being able to effectively communicate. My voice was weak and painfully slow. Almost from the beginning, neither parent nurtured dependence. My dad pushed me to excel, always harder than my mom did.

My rehabilitation began early in March, before the sheepskin commenced its journey to become yellow or thinned. Maple trees in our front yard budded, and robins pulled strings to make nests. I followed sweet lilac smells from our backyard that led me over drain pipes in an effort to evade a young, redheaded physical therapist. I was easy prey, and she proceeded to coerce scores of sit-ups from my atrophied abdominal muscles. Eventually I was able to sit up straight, and the luxury of reclining was laid to rest. When I was able to sit, and even stand assisted, formal therapy began at the University of Minnesota. At the Department of Physical Medicine and Rehabilitation I went through a few months of physical, occupational and speech therapy. Most of it was outpatient. I knew I was going home, safe in my bed with a side rail on it. I vaguely remember a week or two at the university hospital on the inside. Fragments of that time fester suppressed, regressively halcyon in my mind. They are of long nights and even longer days. They are of painfully insecure beds and a patient with a spinal chord injury named Naomi who wore a halo. The department was also used to train student therapists and resident doctors. They were the therapeutic and Hippocratic zealots that pressed sharp plastic goniometers (a physical therapy instrument that measures angles) to my hips and malleoli (the bony prominence on each side of the ankle) to record flexion. The only notable impressions they left on me were in ink.

I walked parallel bars infinitely. I plodded along like a donkey after a carrot behind a giant red contraption that ran electronically along tracks on the therapy gym's ceiling. With great concentration, I buttoned strips of cloth together on boards in occupational therapy. I once produced a copper impression of an old car. It was mounted on a green board, and I pounded out the car in O.T. In speech therapy a metronome clicked at its slowest speed as I mumbled in phonetics.

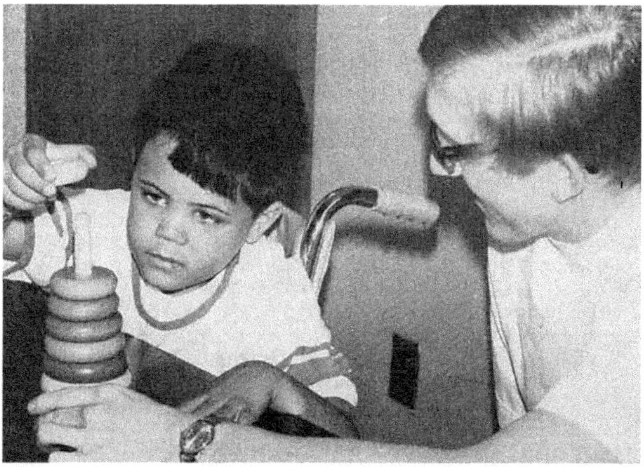

Ψ

War gets uglier when it's allowed to ferment. It stews in its blood until coagulants form armies. Combatants succumb to their basest instincts. On February 1, 1971, the war machine paused to look at what it had become. Vietnam Veterans Against the War members convened at a Howard Johnson's in Detroit for a conference called "The Winter Soldier Investigation." The VVAW had long believed that American troops—the substitutes in a proxy war—were recurrently committing war crimes. It was the intention of Lieutenant John Kerry and Jane Fonda, notably, to raise public awareness of those crimes. One soldier testified:

"Fighting in the war was terrible enough-I shot people-but I never saw any atrocities against civilians. The Viet Cong hung up tribal chiefs and disemboweled them in front of their own families-they did that to their own people. I never saw Americans do anything like that." -Steve Pitkin, Winter Soldier Investigation, January 31, 1971.

Leaders of the conference were able to extract statements from members who witnessed incidents of rape, brutality and racism. The truth or falsehood of many of the statements is contentious and may have been coerced only to advance the VVAW's agenda. What has been ascertained is that in March 1968, personnel of the US Army Americal Division descended upon the tiny village of My Lai in South Central Vietnam. The division had orders to burn the village. The suspicion was that its residents were Viet Cong sympathizers. The inlets consisted of rice paddies, irrigation ditches and dikes. The brigade knew the villagers were going to market the morning of March 16. Tu Cung is a part of the village of My Lai. It is a quiet hamlet with a common area into which Second Lieutenants William Calley and Stephan Brooks herded more than three hundred men, women and children. The leaders ordered their respective platoons to open fire on the unarmed civilians. Women threw themselves on children. When the children got up to walk, Calley shot at them. After the massacre of hundreds, the Americal Division burned the village of My Lai. The incident was not made public in the states until 1969, and the revelation strengthened the anti-war movement.

Later Kerry testified before a Senate committee, citing many of the atrocities he witnessed during his service between 1968 and 1969:

"We who have come here to Washington have come here because we feel we have to be winter soldiers now. We could come back to this country; we could be quiet; we could hold our silence; we could not tell what went on in Vietnam, but we feel because of what threatens this country, the fact that crimes threaten it, not reds, and not redcoats but the crimes which we are committing that threaten it, that we have to speak out."[3]

Ψ

I was still reclining in the chair when my mom organized a second party at our house. My guests were destined to be estranged. They played Don't Break the Ice and Don't Spill the Beans. Propped in the chair, I watched them tap at plastic ice blocks with a small wooden hammer. Or they guardedly set beans on a pot's lid. The pot was suspended on swivels so the beans had to be placed in a liberal distribution or the pot spilled them. One present at that belated sixth birthday party was a Lone Ranger set. There was a mask, a tan Stetson hat and a silver revolver and holster. My mom usually steered us away from guns and other violent toys. She said nothing because the gun was used by a fictional character that fought for justice. More likely it was because it was a gesture that made me happy.

Ψ

Buried deep in deadened days of my first childhood, peeking culpably from the veils of jack-o-lantern plants, shuffled in the antitheses of boxes of literature, cowering behind trash cans set on the small rocks of our back alley, there was gun play. When there were no roads to grade, new earth to taste or pretend *Star Trek* beam ups, I heard the sputters of Tommyguns as my comrades or I fell. I was the indulgent disciple of the older kid next door. For me then, majority ruled. My best friend joined their army, and I was a peering face in the cross-fire. Their parents did not discourage gun play. If they even knew about it. They did not encourage it either. My parents never gave me anything that might lead me to that kind of play. If they knew, and had tried to stop me from the reindeer games, I might have rebelled just to spite them. They played it cool. They let me be a kid. (Incidentally, two of those kids grew up and chose to go in the military).

Ψ

The friends at my party had known me for the first five years and eleven months of my life. I had been absent from their comprehensible worlds for the last two months. Adequate compensation for that time was never found. They were the kids who had comprised those musty autumn séances. They'd been my comrades who smelled the silky hair of the girl as she spun us into oblivion (years later a woman from the neighborhood put together a reunion. Susan and I were the only ones who attended it).

I was pushed in a chair, or I crawled, across rust colored shag carpeting, negotiating my way around a white hassock in the center of the living room. We needed a bigger house, one with fewer obstacles to negotiate. In the early winter of 1972, when my dad and I began our winter walks again in the heated garage, a bigger house was found. It was located about three blocks away, yet Aldrich Avenue might as well have been three miles away. For $47,000 my parents purchased a much larger, single-story house with an attached two-car garage. I could no longer cross with the relative obliviousness a residential street provides. Traffic frequency condensed fifteen minute lapses into seconds. Cars and trucks sped by at thirty-five to forty miles per hour. Our new house stood with mild conspicuousness across Lyndale Avenue at the end of 71st Street. A large sliding glass patio door was between two smaller doors, one real and one for show. The house was sided with aluminum, eliminating my dad's yearly painting of one side of the house.

Amid the terraced, fenced and bay windowed homes aligning Lyndale and Augsburg Avenues, ours had a few idiosyncrasies. Perhaps only for symmetry, it had a faux door to the right of the big sliding window. A visitor did use this door once. The house featured blue lights high in the corners of the façade. The hard beige stucco wall in the foyer and the steps to a small stage always looked like a band shell. Cars went by, glancing if something was happening. Rarely was there a reason to stop. Ken Tilsen, the lawyer retained to handle our lawsuit against the teenage driver, approached our new home in the winter of 1972 bearing a mezuzah. My dad affixed it to the door frame to the left of the window at the customary tilt. Tilsen blessed it: "May this house be safe from tigers."

The house was safe from tigers and distracted teenage drivers, although once a Jehovah's Witness did approach it.

Chapter Eight

When Cats Walk

Typically voters attend their local precinct caucus merely to support a specific candidate. In 1968's third district precinct caucus Fred Amram raised his hand and volunteered to go to the following level—the state senate district convention. Here all the precinct delegates of a senate district convene to endorse state House of Representatives and State Senate candidates and to elect delegates to send to the congressional district convention. Many committees are formed and meetings are scheduled between each level. By the congressional district level, Amram had attained a standing as a leader in the third district among the Dissident Democrats, if not the DFL Party as a whole, and he sought a delegate position to the next two levels—the state and national conventions. In the spring of 1968, he was elected as delegate to the national convention in Chicago that summer.

Ψ

A Sabbath—if we observed it at all—was celebrated according to the Reform practice of Judaism. Our Sabbaths were brief and largely improvised. On August 23 it occurred at 8:06 p.m. and Friday faded into the sunset as it did for any Jewish family. We tore off formidable hunks of challah after saying Hamotzi to bless the bread. The adults sipped wine following the requisite Kiddish prayer. My dad anticipated sleeping late Saturday. A plane ticket from Minneapolis to Chicago had been purchased in advance. A bag was packed for a four-day trip and waited by the door ready to leave Sunday for the Democratic National Convention, although so far 1968's story had been as twisted as the challah loaf before us.

I was restless. Having had practice appeasing babysitters, I was also accomplished at feigning sleep. Somewhere in our house a phone rang. It was allowed to ring three to six times before it was answered. I waited for muffles to fade to drones. Eventually my mom's voice broke the silence, and footsteps approached the room I shared with my sister. I dove for cover. Slowly the covers parted, and my eyes settled on a line of light under the door. I watched Mushy's—our stray cat—shadow cross my mom's path. She popped her head in the room, and I squirmed under the covers again, clutching my dog-eared panda bear tighter. My sister, genuinely asleep, turned over and rubbed her eyes. My mom delivered her news.

"Opa has had a serious heart attack. He may not make it through the night."

Opa was already dead, but my mom was delicate, if not forthright. My dad had always told us to expect him to have a heart attack at sixty-three.[1] He studied the genetics and calculated his future. He looked identical to his father and shared a vigilant work ethic. Milton Amram, my Opa, had his first heart attack in 1964. He was sixty-three. The doctor told Milton to lighten his work load. In 1967 his heart attacked him again. His doctor advised him to ease up and to watch his salt intake. He briefly attempted to curb his ways, but soon he was back on his Fuller Brush route in South Jersey.

Milton and Sitta had been living in Red Bank, New Jersey since 1959. When their "Freddy" was married and had begun a life in Minnesota, they finally left New York City. Beginning in the summer of 1944, Milton had commuted from their Manhattan apartment on 77th street. His day began at four a.m. He walked to the subway that he rode to Penn station. From there he boarded a train that went to a platform in South Jersey where he parked his car each night. He proceeded to drive his route though through towns such as Freehold and Matawan.

Susan knew that a funeral awaited us. At three years old, all I really knew was the adventure a plane trip can offer. My sister helped pack a bag for both of us. My mom quickly added some things to my dad's bag for herself. A taxi had been dispatched for us, and it arrived promptly and ghostly, coasting to a stop at our curb. I leaned my crew cut head out the door. It bristled in the breeze, and I listened to crickets that offered an ominous tranquility to the night. Our cab driver honked once or twice, and the four of us proceeded boldly into the night.

A full-size commercial airplane took us to Newark, New Jersey. It slid through the night, and I closed my eyes to tease sleep. A jarring landing woke me. From the tarmac at Newark's airport we climbed, quite literally, into a small single-engine plane. As it lifted clumsily into dawn's skyline, I noticed how our luggage was jammed tight, and seating was limited. The small craft chopped its way through the short flight, the constant turbulence foreshadowing that which awaited my dad in Chicago.

We arrived at Oma's apartment late Saturday morning. In spite of the circumstances it appeared to have been cleaned. My paternal grandmother was hysterical and spent many hours crying. My mom comforted her, producing that calming, conducive counsel that is prone to slide easily from the arms of social workers. It was clear to me then that Opa was gone, but then you really can't miss a person that you never really knew. A picture is evidence that we spent at least one time together. All I'm certain of is that he was a gentle and quiet man who once bought me an ice cream at the Dairy Queen on Lyndale Avenue when I was two.

By Jewish Law, the Sabbath is not for funerals so Saturday was spent listening to Oma contemplating her life without Opa through intermittent sobs. Susan and I entertained ourselves with a balloon. Sunday arrived, and the five of us piled into Opa's car. A tiny building served as a funeral home. The room was distinctly Semitic in its daily aura. It was clearly a multi-purpose room, obliged to be interchangeable. On sunday August 25 it was required to cater a Jewish funeral. It was a parlor with small chambers to conceal mourners like the spaces in kugel[2] where raisins hide. The room begged for more space. Milton's sister Beda and her second husband Chil attended. Chil's daughter Mona was there. A handful of fellow brush men milled in a corner of the room. Cigar smoke smell mingled with the odious tendencies of the room's changing hands. A few of Milton's customers paid respect to their Fuller Brush man. One or two refugee families from the old country tried to give some authenticity to the proceedings. A hired rabbi really did not know anything about Milton. His words were generic and trite and emphasized the fact that Milton was a refugee of the Holocaust called to what lies beyond this world. Milton Amram is buried in Beth Israel Cemetery in Woodbridge, New Jersey—a city twenty-three miles north of Red Bank.

After the funeral, in the absence of Shiva reflections, the recouping of the momentous physical forces that his father's death had sired, my dad's focus reverted back to the continuing story of Eugene J. McCarthy. He distanced himself from dealing with the loss of his father and went into a room. A small black and white TV set tuned in images of peaceful protesters gathering in Chicago for the convention. Vice President Hubert Humphrey had arrived that afternoon to massive opposition from his own party. Placards favoring Gene McCarthy surrounded him as his staff ushered him in from the tarmac. Humphrey's staff wondered whether the vice president could hold his party together long enough to win the nomination. Senator McCarthy had also arrived in Chicago that afternoon and addressed his legions of supporters. Yippie leaders Abbie Hoffman and Jerry Rubin were threatening to lace the city's water supply with LSD and hold mass nude swimming in Lake Michigan if the city officials did not grant them permits to demonstrate. The event they promoted was called "The Festival of Life." Another group of demonstrators, led by Tom Hayden, Rennie Davis and David Dellinger, planned a peaceful demonstration in Grant Park.

Milton's death came at the climax of his son's political involvement for McCarthy. The convention was the dénouement, and Opa's funeral threatened the rising action that had been building since McCarthy's story began nine months earlier. After the funeral, a second plane ticket to Chicago was purchased. My dad said his goodbyes to us and his grieving mother on Monday. He boarded a bus to the Newark airport and arrived in Chicago on August 27. He checked in the Hilton where many of the McCarthy delegates stayed. He mingled in the lobby with Don Fraser, apprising himself of the day's proceedings, including the brutality in the streets that, to him, may have had an insidious familiarity.

Ψ

On the morning of August 22, a Sioux Indian from South Dakota dressed in hippie garb. Heavily armed Chicago police alleged that the Native American had fired the first shot. They surrounded the seventeen year old and killed him on Wells Street. Later that day a memorial march was organized by Yippies.

Hello Delegates
Welcome to
CHICAGO
Richard Daley

A convention hat's blue, white and red band read: "Mayor Richard J. Daley." A hand tipping it poked up from the corner of the sign. In Lincoln and Grant Park more than 5,500 Illinois

National Guardsmen waited nervously for the convention to begin. 'Daley dozers' graded Chicago's streets. They hummed softly and deceptively, anticipating protesters becoming enmeshed on the jeeps' barb-wired bumpers. Uniformed officers were on every street corner armed with helmets, batons, tear gas, mace and gas masks. Squad cars patrolled downtown streets, each provided one shotgun. Police were on the rooftop and in the corridors of the Conrad Hilton Hotel. The hotel hosted Vice President Humphrey and Senator McCarthy. Sentries were posted outside the candidates' suites twenty-four hours a day (the "happy warrior" received six death threats during the convention). Everyone entering or exiting the elevators was asked to show identification. Across the street at the Sheraton Blackstone Hotel, Senator George McGovern received similar security. Chain-linked fence topped with barbed wire encompassed the International Amphitheater. Inside, high above the convention floor, was a cat-walk that armed guards paced. Tanks were parked on Michigan Avenue like watchdogs, and police were on their leashes. Because my dad missed the convention's first day he did not have the credentials necessary to gain access to the convention. He approached the amphitheater and was questioned by security. When he could not prove his purpose there, armed guards picked him up under the arms and carried him, his suitcase and briefcase far from the theater (at least a quarter mile separated the theater and the chain-link fence). Finally the security guards allowed my dad to call into the amphitheater by phone. He contacted Warren Spannaus—head of Minnesota's McCarthy delegation—who brought out the credentials.

Ψ

Anti-American sentiment had lingered among the South Vietnamese for over a year. Saigon reported that students, professors, journalists and Buddhists believed the US had rigged the election of their president, General Nguyên Văn Thiêu. Ellsworth Bunker's (ambassador to Saigon) deputy Eugene M. Locke argued that Americans were winning. He claimed the US was succeeding in games with the Vietnamese mind, basing his argument on signs of dissension within North Vietnamese and Viet Cong ranks. Locke confirmed his argument, saying "The enemy is losing control of the people for his side. His recruitment has dropped off sharply…"[3]

Eugene Locke cited documents he had gathered from Saigon. They were translated by the CIA and subject to misinterpretation. A letter documented an August 8, 1967 meeting attended by twenty-eight key Viet Cong personnel. Yielded from the meeting were seven problems that indicated the opposition was tired of the war:

- The majority of Viet Cong soldiers in the Giong Trom district were tired of the longevity of the war.
- The personnel were afraid of air strikes, artillery and M-113 armored personnel carriers.
- Key officers did not want to work harder to train guerrillas.
- A majority of Viet Cong soldiers robbed or oppressed civilians.
- Many of the Viet Cong were undisciplined. They used weapons to kill each other and had caused dissension within the units.
- Most Viet Cong officials lacked political dedication.
- The consensus of VC soldiers felt they were not able to defeat the government of Vietnam or the Allies.

Dr. Henry Kissinger, a Harvard professor serving as informal consultant and mediator for the White House, had been orchestrating contacts throughout the "summer of love." He'd been aiding negotiations between North Vietnamese diplomat Mai Van Bo and two French civilians, one of whom was an old friend of Ho Chi Minh.

The negotiations were known as the "San Antonio formula." It was a reference to a speech the president had delivered there September 29, 1967. In the speech he had offered to cease the bombing of North Vietnam if Ho Chi Minh agreed to negotiations. Now, Kissinger negotiated, via telephone, with a third-world country's leader. Johnson also wanted the North Vietnamese president to promise not to use the bombing reprieve as a chance to bolster the troops and supplies into South Vietnam. The leader never responded.

At the beginning of 1968 Robert Kennedy had no intention of seeking the Democratic nomination. His staff advised that successfully running against an incumbent president was unrealistic. A week after the Tet Offensive began, January 31, Kennedy spoke in Chicago. His "Unwinnable War" speech focused on the delusion the American government had created to convince itself (and the young men fighting the war) that victory in Vietnam was attainable. The speech signaled Kennedy's clear break from any complicity with the president's policies in Southeast Asia. Later that month Kennedy received a letter from journalist Peter Hamill. The letter stated America's poor kept pictures of his brother on their walls. Its message conveyed the idea that the New York senator had "an obligation of staying true to whatever it was that put those pictures on those walls."[3] Inspired by the letter, Kennedy traveled to Delano, California to meet with civil rights activist César Chávez. Chávez, who represented America's poor migrant farm workers, was on a twenty-five-day hunger strike. During this visit, the senator, possibly inspired by Chávez's show of commitment to non-violent protest, decided to challenge the incumbent Johnson. On the weekend before the New Hampshire primary Kennedy made it clear to his staff that he wanted McCarthy to step away from the race to avoid splitting the anti-war vote. After the primary, Kennedy publicly announced his candidacy on March 16. Among the first to endorse Kennedy was Speaker of the California State Assembly, Jesse Unruh.

Ψ

"I shall not seek, and I will not accept, the nomination of my party for another term as your president. But let men everywhere know, however, that a strong, a confident, and a vigilant America stands ready tonight to seek an honorable peace and stands ready tonight to defend an honored cause-whatever the price, whatever the burden, whatever the sacrifice that duty may require..."[4]

Four days later, on April 4, Martin Luther King Jr. was assassinated. That night Robert Kennedy was campaigning in Indiana. The senator prepared a speech for delivery to a preponderantly black audience. The city's chief of police warned Kennedy that his remarks could incite riots, and they were not able to guarantee his protection. The senator proceeded boldly:

"For those of you who are black and are tempted to be filled with hatred and mistrust of the injustice of such an act, against all white people, I would only say that I can feel in my own heart the same kind of feeling. I had a member of my family killed, but he was killed by a white man."

His words, from the back of a pick-up truck, are credited, in part, for preventing rioting in Indianapolis. Post-assassination riots engulfed the streets of Minneapolis and more than one hundred other cities. The Democratic Party splintered further.

- One group consisted of labor unions. These were the parties controlled by big-city bosses, such as Mayor Daley. They had controlled the party since the days of FDR and now rallied to support Humphrey.
- Students and older professionals who had always opposed the war formed their own grouping. They were the people who, like the dissident delegates, truly believed they were the future of the Democratic Party.

- Another group now attracted Catholics, blacks and other minorities. They were anti-war and supported Robert Kennedy (after RFK's assassination, many from this group supported George McGovern).
- There was a group made up of older Democrats. It included former "Dixiecrats" who remembered the positive impact Roosevelt's New Deal had on the South. Many chose to support Humphrey, although a few chose the third-party candidate, George Wallace.

Primaries were held in South Dakota, California and New Jersey on June 4. Robert Kennedy scored slight victories over McCarthy in two of the races—California 46 percent to 42 percent and South Dakota 50 percent to 20 percent. The next night, as he prepared to address supporters at Los Angeles's Ambassador Hotel, Kennedy was fatally shot. A great loss was felt by all. For dissident Democrats, though, the grief was bifurcated. They felt the well-known New York Senator Kennedy had taken the success of the comparatively unknown Minnesota senator. Kennedy had coasted on a wave of political primary success that McCarthy had started. Gene had been in the trenches; *he* had shaken hands and spoken to supporters."Bobby" was a Kennedy after all. He did not want or need to do all the grassroots campaigning. In March, after McCarthy had great success in the New Hampshire primary, it was apparent to Kennedy that defeating an incumbent president *was* realistic. As for Humphrey, the assassination all but guaranteed him the nomination. He was deeply shaken by the news about his opponent. The vice president returned to his home in Minnesota for two weeks during which he met with Johnson. At the time of Kennedy's assassination, the delegate totals were:

- Hubert Humphrey- 561
- Robert Kennedy- 393
- Eugene McCarthy- 258

Even with Humphrey's inheritance of many Kennedy delegates he still trailed Senator McCarthy in some popular opinion polls. The once forthright advocate of civil rights felt the sting of boos from protesters when fifty thousand greeted him at a June 24 solidarity march for civil rights at the Lincoln Memorial. Hostile anti-war crowds were often encountered where Humphrey campaigned. Frustrated, he tried to move out of the president's shadow. He tried to distance himself from the policies on the war Johnson had held him to for so long. Late in June he asked Johnson if he could deviate from the administration's war policies. The vice president offered a plan that included ending Operation Rolling Thunder and the withdrawal of military personnel. Johnson was adamant on staying the course and claimed that deviation from it could impede the peace process. He warned that Humphrey's breaking with policy endangered the lives of American soldiers. The vice president was even threatened with having the blood of Johnson's son-in-law, Charles Robb (US Marine Corps 1961 to 1970), on his hands.[5] Humphrey criticized McCarthy's constant attacks on the administration's war policy. He said the senator really offered no plausible plan. In July McCarthy challenged the vice president to several debates on various issues including the war. Humphrey took the challenge, although he limited it to a single debate prior to the Democratic National Convention. The pairing never occurred, largely because of concern for hostilities stemming from the Eastern Bloc invasion of Czechoslovakia.[6]

A plan, orchestrated by Jesse Unruh and Mayor Daley, aimed to draft Senator Edward Kennedy for the presidential nomination. The junior senator from Massachusetts rejected the idea. The vice president's advisors thought that having a Kennedy on the ticket would be beneficial in the general election. The plan was to let the liberalism of a Kennedy remove the hawkish mantle Johnson had cast over his vice president. Kennedy rejected the offer.

Shortly after Robert Kennedy's assassination, South Dakota senator George McGovern (a supporter of Kennedy) was considered to fill the vacancy. In August, after assuring himself that Edward was not a candidate, McGovern announced his bid for the Democratic party's nomination. By doing so he said he was committing himself to goals for which "Kennedy had given his life." When asked why he should get the nomination of his party he replied simply, "Well, Gene doesn't really want to be president, and I do."[7]

1968 Democratic Presidential Primaries

Date	State	McCarthy	Johnson	Kennedy
3/12/68	NH	42%	50%	1%
4/2/68	WI	56%	35%	6%
4/23/68	PA	71%	4%	11%
4/30/68	MA	49%	3%	28%
5/5/68	DC	0%	0%	0%
5/7/68	IN	27%	42%	0%
5/7/68	OH	0%	0%	0%
5/14/68	NE	31%	6%	52%
5/14/68	WV	0%	0%	0%
5//28/68	FL	29%	0%	0%
5/28/68	OR	44%	12%	38%
6/4/68	CA	42%	46%	0%
6/4/68	NJ	36%	31%	0%
6/4/68	SD	20%	30%	50%
6/11/68	IL	39%	1%	0%

Throughout April, speculation of Humphrey's bid for the nomination had dominated headlines. Finally, at the end of the month, Humphrey confirmed his candidacy. He won the most delegates of the campaign during a six-week period in which the war was briefly removed as a contentious issue due to peace talks with Hanoi. The vice president had never competed in a primary race himself and began using "favorite son"[8] candidates as surrogates to weaken his opponents. He won fifty-seven delegates from Florida with George Smathers defeating McCarthy in the primary with 46 percent of the vote.

Johnson-Humphrey Surrogates

Candidate	Popular Vote	% of Populace
Sen. Stephen M. Young (D-OH)	549,140	7.30
Thomas C. Lynch (Attorney General-CA)	380, 286	5.05
Gov. Roger D. Branigin (D-IN)	238,700	3.17
Sen. George Smathers (D-FL)	236,242	3.14
Scott Kelly	128,899	1.71

Hubert Humphrey II—the son of a pharmacist—was said to hold a "drug store" view of the world, prompting critics to question his capacity to be president. After earning his pharmacist's license, Hubert helped his father run the family drugstore from 1931 to 1937. Publicly and privately the vice president had referenced the store as the basis of his decisions. He'd grown up in the drought-torn Dakotas with his father often struggling to keep his business. The realities experienced growing up influenced his politics and he expressed those realities in his approach to Communism. He felt a loyalty to Johnson. He shared the president's apprehensions of the domino theory but also wanted to be the champion of civil rights McCarthy supporters remembered.

Ever since the 1964 Democratic National Convention, when Lyndon Johnson had urged Democrats to select the Senate Democratic Whip as the vice presidential nominee, Hubert Humphrey was dominated by Johnson and his policies. Humphrey's loyal nature and an abysmal aspiration to be president made him vulnerable as a pawn of the president. At a press conference in the summer of 1968 he was asked how his position differed from Johnson in reference to Vietnam. Because Johnson was no longer a candidate for president, Humphrey refused to repudiate him. Johnson carried a fair amount of leverage on the nomination process. If Humphrey had chosen not to support the president's policy on the war, it is unlikely he would have received Johnson's endorsement. He was silenced and blinded by his own ambition to be president—so much so that he failed to appreciate the force of opposition within his own party.

Ψ

In June, at the DFL state convention, McCarthy's recent win in the New York primary added to the optimism. Supporters were invigorated, and their hopes for a national win were strengthened. That feeling was somewhat diminished when it was discovered that the New York State Democratic Committee allowed the Minnesota senator only fifteen and a half votes from the sixty-five delegates at-large. Still, McCarthy was changing the opinion of the media. The *Minneapolis Star* reconsidered the winner of the Democratic nomination:

"A year of political surprises has produced another—the strong showing of Eugene McCarthy forces in New York. The Minnesota senator keeps campaigning in the face of 'expert' opinion that he hasn't a chance. Maybe the Democratic presidential nomination isn't in Vice-president Humphrey's lap yet."

Confidence followed McCarthy delegates to the state convention even though polls showed Humphrey *did* have the Minnesota State Convention delegates in his pocket. Twenty of the at-large delegates went to him. That meant, by the national convention, he'd have enough votes to win the nomination. Of the 1,119 votes, Humphrey had over 600. McCarthy had a little more than 500. A headline predicted the winner: "HHH backers expect he'll be nominated."

The *Minneapolis Star* reported that the Humphrey campaign attained the balance of power within the party as it shifted following Robert Kennedy's assassination. It estimated that Humphrey had 1,811 delegate votes to McCarthy's 502. The *New York Times* reported that the vice-president had more than the 1,312 delegate votes needed for the nomination.

Following the DFL state convention Allard Lowenstein had a plan to block the nomination of the vice president and boost McCarthy's candidacy. On June 29, 1,200 disaffected Democrats met in Chicago. Chiefly organized by Lowenstein, they were the Coalition for an Open Convention. The plan to mount a fourth-party bid for the nomination was canceled. Lowenstein said that it was too late in the race for that. The dissidents were unclear what their course of action would be if Humphrey did not win the nomination. Lowenstein joked that if they came to that bridge he would jump off it. He met privately with Senator McCarthy and explained his plans. He said that to implement it, he needed to enlist the 461 delegate voters who had pledged support to Senator Kennedy. Lowenstein also intended to get the votes of blacks who had supported Kennedy. The convention consisted of a series of small caucuses, each focusing on a different constituency. Lowenstein stressed the need to unseat delegates whose election had violated democratic procedures. There was a caucus for the Fourth Party. There was a caucus for a conglomeration of lawyers. There was a Delegate Caucus, two black caucuses, and a Kennedy Caucus. As the pre-convention block concluded, there was an "On to Chicago Caucus." If nothing else, Lowenstein's mini-convention gave confidence to student supporters of McCarthy.

Kenneth Tilsen, a lawyer for Minnesota's Concerned Democrats, was in Chicago a week prior to the convention as part of the credentials committee. On Wednesday, August 21, Tilsen met with 110 others on the committee chaired by New Jersey Governor Richard Hughes. The Minnesota lawyer was there to ensure the McCarthy delegates were heard from equally and the balloting was judicious. He spoke colorfully. He blurred a thin line between sarcasm and respect, describing the Conrad Hilton as an armed fortress. Tilsen "approached a tribunal of robed priests who allowed him to speak his heresy about their pope, Hubert H. Humphrey." He mused about a priest rising from his seat, a halo flashing in the light, and the priest condemning him a heretic. Tilsen was escorted out of the castle, at which time he sought his escape to Minnesota. He said he watched the battle unfold on television, safe in his home.

Senator Daniel Inouye, D-Hawaii, delivered the keynote speech. Vice President Humphrey was nominated for president on the first ballot. Senator Edmund Muskie of Maine received the vice presidential nomination. Roughly three hundred leaderless Kennedy delegates had backed George McGovern. Black protest candidate Channing Phillips, leader of a delegation from the District of Columbia, collected many of the delegates that had been pledged to Kennedy. At the convention's roll call the South Dakota senator came in third:

Hubert H. Humphrey	1,760
Eugene J. McCarthy	601
George S. McGovern	146
Channing Phillips	68

On Wednesday, August 28, with anti-war protesters gathered outside the Chicago Hilton mouthing "The whole world is watching," Jesse Unruh voiced his endorsement of Senator Eugene McCarthy from the convention floor. The endorsement was a concession. Unruh's true intent was to endorse a Kennedy to heed the anti-war cause.

Irony came in the thrust of police batons. Demonstrators were herded into police vans and were subject to a "superfluous whack of a nightstick."[9] Daley, who'd aligned with Unruh for a Kennedy, denied most permits to demonstrate the week of the convention. Anti-war groups petitioned the city. A single permit was allowed for a rally on the third day of the convention. It allowed fifteen thousand students to gather at the old band shell at the south end of Grant Park. Following the rally, attempts were made to approach the International Amphitheater. Thousands of protesters were thwarted by police as they neared the Conrad Hilton Hotel. Scores of arrests were made, mostly for damage to private property. Television networks intermittently cut away from the convention proceedings to cover the violence outside. Police were injured as well as the marchers. Often, journalists covering the actions had their cameras smashed and the film confiscated.

The day bled into night, and tear gas bled into the Conrad Hilton. The gas disturbed the vice president in his suite high above the Windy City. As he tendered his acceptance speech, demonstrators on Michigan Avenue were kept under control by the National Guard. Safe inside, delegates voted on the peace plank. A plank to abolish the unit rule failed, and a vote was passed to keep it until 1972.[10] The anti-war resolution was also defeated. The minority report flashed on a monitor. It hung, tauntingly resistant to reason, in the center of the convention center.

CBS News Tabulation
Platform Challenge: Vietnam Plank

Yes	1,041
NO	1,567.5
NEEDED TO PASS	1,311.5

It was a prompter rigged to mute the voices that had for so long called for an end to the war.

The news brought tears to the eyes of some McCarthy delegates. The math of the numbers was only calculable one way. Their sum figured that the war would continue indefinitely. I imagine the awesome feeling of defeat, how many must have felt that all the work, all the impetus that had buoyed them to Chicago to turn the direction of the war was for naught. The convention, for all intents and purposes, was over. Peace had lost. The democratic process had failed. Soon the delegates on the convention floor broke into "We shall overcome," and they waved a banner that simply read, "STOP THE WAR." Across the aisle, Humphrey's supporters were jubilant. A brass band stuck up "Happy days are here again," drowning out the McCarthy crowd's vows to overcome.

The vice president had realized a life-long dream. He approached the final hurdle to the presidency. Thursday night, as violent parries between students and blue-collar policemen emboldened, he prepared to deliver his acceptance speech. Many of McCarthy's delegates from other states walked out in protest, although the delegation from Minnesota, feeling a sense of allegiance to him as a native son, stayed for Humphrey's speech. He began by expressing his gratification in his achievement and acknowledging the violence taking place outside the theater as he spoke. He mused on traditions of Franklin Roosevelt, Harry Truman, Adlai Stevenson and John F. Kennedy. He praised Lyndon Johnson for rallying America when it was grief-stricken. He spoke about Johnson accomplishing more "unfinished business of America than any modern predecessor."[11] His words were designed to secure Johnson a favorable legacy. Even Humphrey's limelight drew Johnson's shadow.

Final Tallies

Presidential	Vice Presidential
Hubert Humphrey—1,759	Edmund Muskie—1,943
Eugene McCarthy—601	Not Voting—604
George McGovern—146	Julian Bond—49
Channing Phillips—68	David Hoeh—4
Daniel More—17	Edward Kennedy—3
Edward Kennedy—13	Eugene McCarthy—4
George Wallace—0.5	
James Gray—0.5	
Paul Bryant—2	Others—16

Ronnie Kaibel, wife of Fifth Congressional District delegate Howie Kaibel, questioned the worth of the convention. She questioned her husband's and other delegates' participation in a convention that "almost from the first day seemed to me to be undemocratic."[12]

Late in evenings, after the convention sessions ended, McCarthy delegates crossed the street to Grant Park to talk with demonstrators. One night John Galbraith was talking to the protesters. Alpha Smaby said she empathized with them. They looked at her blankly, with a sense of wonderment that begged the question how she, Galbraith or any of the delegates to the convention still saw the importance of what they were doing there. Smaby walked along Michigan Avenue looking deeply into the dead stares of guardsmen brandishing rifles. She suddenly realized that there must be a sickness within the Democratic Party to allow such injustice to happen.

Connecticut senator Abraham Ribicoff, in his nomination of George McGovern, spoke of the violence occurring in the streets of America. "With George McGovern we wouldn't have Gestapo tactics on the streets of Chicago..."[13] The most biting sounds were censored for the world as it watched. However, critics later claimed that lip-readers could make out the words synced from Daley's lips during Ribicoff's speech. "Fuck you, you Jew son-of-a-bitch! You lousy motherfucker! Go home!" Sometimes the quivering and anguished lips of sniveling bigots say the most.

Donald Heffernan, an alternate from Minnesota's Fourth District, was safe inside the amphitheater. Those with active roles in the convention were spared the spectacle, for instance, of a woman being thrown through a plate glass window. Heffernan's wife Mary spoke of "pools of blood" in the foyer of the Hilton. She recalled riding with a young black man during the riot. As he navigated his vehicle through the clouds of tear-gas, he told her there was a lesson here. He asserted that the riots and tear-gas gave white people an idea of what a black citizen could be subjected to any given day. McCarthy Democrats were dissidents that challenged the established policy of how war was approached in America. The violence in Chicago that week was aimed—for the most part—at young white protesters. It was appallingly reminiscent of what happened when black protesters attempted to cross a Selma, AL bridge only three years earlier.[14]

Early on Friday morning Chicago police stormed the fifteenth floor of the Hilton. Some of the McCarthy staff and volunteers were brutalized by police. They were dragged downstairs, some in their pajamas, for questioning. The police accused the alleged offenders of throwing tables and ashtrays out of the window. The young staffers shivered in fear in the hotel lobby. Finally, Senator McCarthy was called from his suite on the twenty-third floor. He assessed the situation, its false accusations and unwarranted seizures. Only two were injured seriously in the incident. By the convention's end there were 668 arrests made. The city's hospitals reported treating 111 demonstrators. In Vietnam, during the week of the convention,

308 Americans were killed and 1,144 were wounded—no victors claimed the spoils of two wars.

Abbie Hoffman, Jerry Rubin, Tom Hayden, Rennie Davis, John Froines, David Dellinger and Lee Weiner gained media attention as "The Chicago Seven." In March of 1969 they were charged with inciting a riot and anything relevant to counter-cultural protests that took place during the convention. The eighth man charged, Bobby Seale, had been severed from the case during the initial proceedings. Seale's outbursts in court had caused him to be bound and gagged in his chair. The Yippies' (Youth International Party) only intent had been to bring over one hundred thousand young people to Chicago for five days of peace and love. The intent was to create a bridge connecting youth culture and music to meet political ends. The Yippies set out to create a story of what *could* happen in Chicago. They intended to create a story so amazing and contrary to popular opinion that the media notified the world of it. A youth movement, over one hundred thousand strong, acted out a story in the streets of Chicago. It was grassroots organizing—the low man exploiting the media for his own gain. The Yippies' efforts failed in the end because Daley did not grant them a permit.

The festival's sign depicted all fifty states fragmented in puzzle pieces.

FESTIVAL OF LIFE
Aug. 25-30, CHICAGO
MUSIC-LIGHTS-FREE-THEATER-MAGIC

"I pointed out that it was in the best interests of the city to have us in Lincoln Park, ten miles away from the convention hall. I said we had no intention of marching on the convention hall, that I didn't particularly think that politics in America could be changed by marches and rallies, that we were presenting an alternative lifestyle and we hoped that people of Chicago would come up and mingle in Lincoln Park and see what we were about."- Abbie Hoffman, 1969

During the trial Hoffman ridiculed the judge, noting to Justice Hoffman "you are a shande für die Goyim (a disgrace in front of the Gentiles). You would have served Hitler better," informing him that his idea of justice was the only obscenity in the courtroom. Among those called to testify for the defense were Judy Collins, Arlo Guthrie, "Country" Joe McDonald, Allen Ginsberg, Norman Mailer, Timothy Leary and Reverend Jesse Jackson. The Chicago Seven's attorney was an artist. William Kunstler put the government and the war itself on trial by placing a Viet Cong flag on the defense table. He then donned a black armband to commemorate the dead. As a jury deliberated on the verdict, Judge Hoffman handed down numerous charges of contempt of court to the defendants and their counsel. Sentences ranged from two-and-a-half months to four years.[15]

Ψ

At the end of the convention an insoluble sense of loss plagued many of the McCarthy delegates. Howard Kaibel described the convention as a "terribly depressing week, from beginning to end." However, Fred Amram—a third district delegate from Minnesota—said he was so immersed in the political process that the DFL's loss and the undemocratic overtones of the convention had not registered with him as overtly as it had for some. He said the political system—albeit fractured—was still a democratic system in which he was allowed to participate. Toward the end of the week the loss to the DFL party, as well as the loss of his father, finally came clear to him. "The trip home (from Chicago) was painful. I had come to the convention from the funeral of my father, and my personal loss was intensified by the political loss of the convention."[16] He remembered the pain he felt for the convention's losses and the loss of his father being mixed with pride. Amram knew his father was proud. Milton Amram was proud because his son, a refugee from Nazi Germany (and American citizen since 1945) had a voice at the national level of a democratic system.

Amram's reaction is interesting to me. A majority of McCarthy delegates were greatly disillusioned, demoralized and even outraged by what they experienced. In reference to the police raid on McCarthy headquarters, the senator's wife Abigail wrote, "It puzzles me to this day that so little was made—even in the Walker Report[17]—of the gross and unprecedented suspension of civil liberties. What presidential candidate in our history has had his staff submitted to such indignities?"[18] Amram had come from a childhood of seeing and feeling human injustices and degradation. Now, after escaping those injustices, and a likely death in Germany, he simply appreciated being allowed to take an active role in government. That week Amram was the outsider looking into America. He was a thirty-seven-year-old college professor who'd seen such "Gestapo tactics" before. He tells me the memory did not register with him at the time. I submit that the unconscious images from childhood traumas like Kristallnacht help explain his reaction. I suggest that, to him, a government brutalizing its own citizens in twentieth century America was *not* the anomaly it was to people like Ronnie Kaibel. He had witnessed such brutality thirty years ago in twentieth century Germany.

A train sped away from Middle-America's tiny police state, and a great sigh of relief went through it. The experience at the convention shattered any trust in the government for many. The sight of policemen stirred fear in some for months after the convention. *Minneapolis Star* reporter Ted Smebakken was on the train and remembered people singing and drinking a lot. Humphrey and McCarthy delegates sang "On Wisconsin" as the train approached the border, and they cheered as it left Illinois. Smaby recalled, "The odor of the stink bombs in the Conrad Hilton lingered with me for a long time."[19]

Ψ

In the convention's aftermath the Paris Peace Accords—which had convened in May—were sabotaged. Republican presidential candidate Richard Nixon feared the war could end prior to the general election, robbing him of the option of ending it on his terms. Bryce Harlow, a former staffer in the Eisenhower administration, claimed he had "a double agent"—Henry Kissinger— working in the White House to keep Nixon informed. Kissinger, who became secretary of state under Nixon, claimed to have no political motive. He was neutral in politics and was confident he'd have a job regardless of who became president, Humphrey or Nixon.

Early in 1968, after the unexpected success of anti-war candidate Eugene McCarthy in the New Hampshire primary, Johnson had halted bombing operations in North Vietnam. Kissinger had predicted the reprieve, claiming it was a plan to throw the election to Humphrey. Democratic Senator George Smathers informed the president of the Nixon campaign's knowledge of the plan. In fact, the plan was designed to entice Hanoi to begin negotiations. In May, Hanoi agreed to discuss a total halt to the bombing. At the peace talks, former North Vietnamese Foreign Minister Xuan Thuy headed their delegation. As its ambassador-at-large, the US sent Averell Harriman, who had served as US ambassador to the Soviet Union and to Britain. The talks came to a deadlock at North Vietnam's demand for a halt of US bombing (over two thousand Americans were killed during that first month of peace talks, the highest monthly casualty count of the war).

Nixon had a liaison—Anna Chennault—to South Vietnam president Nguyên Văn Thiêu. On November 2, Chennault informed the South Vietnamese ambassador that her 'boss' told her that he (Nixon) was going to win the election. She told Harriman to request that his boss, Thiêu, "Hold on a while longer."[20] John Mitchell,

Nixon's campaign manager, was getting reports that Thiêu never planned to attend the peace talks.

Johnson knew of Nixon's plans to obstruct the accords. Later, in October, the president saw an opportunity for actions that could begin peace talks again. South Vietnam's president was impeding the peace talks. Two days before Halloween, Johnson learned why the talks had stopped.

Eugene V. Rostow, Johnson's under-secretary of state for political affairs, got word from Wall Street financier Alexander Sacs that one of Nixon's closest financial backers was concocting a plan by his own campaign to block a peace settlement. The information became like a stock tip. It was divulged to other investors over lunch and became a bargaining chip. The backer was in agreement with investors on how to make money with their inside knowledge of Richard Nixon's plan to prolong the war in Vietnam. Rowstow's brother, Walter, the president's national security advisor, was apprised of the information. Walter received a memorandum stating the information had come up in the context of a "professional discussion about the future of financial markets in the near term." It also said that the bearer of this information thought the chances of a cease-fire were small. Eugene said Nixon was 'playing' the problem, trying to block the peace process by instructing Saigon to be difficult and telling Hanoi to wait.

On Halloween night, Thursday October 31, Lyndon Johnson went on national television to announce the halt of the bombing of North Vietnam. The announcement came as a surprise, and the nation thought peace was a treat in the bag.

The New York Times
November 1, 1968

ATTACKS ON NORTH VIETNAM HALT TODAY.
JOHNSON SAYS WIDER TALKS BEGIN NOV. 6

By Saturday November 2, the war was on again. South Vietnam backed out of the deal North Vietnam's president had brokered with Johnson. Thiêu was promised—via Chennault—that a Nixon administration had a better peace deal than a Humphrey administration offered. Saturday morning the *New York Times* headline stated, "U.S.-SAIGON RIFT ON TALKS WIDENS." Its article stated "President Nguyên Văn Thiêu declared that his government would not participate in the Paris talks next week."

A telephone conversation Saturday morning between President Johnson and Richard Russel, chairman of the Senate Committee on Armed Services (D-GA), explains what transpired between October 31 and November 2:

LBJ:	Hello?
Operator:	Go ahead please, sir.
Russell:	Good morning Mr. President.
LBJ:	How are you my friend?
Russell:	Just fine.
LBJ:	Well I've got one this morning that's pretty rough for you. We have found out that our friend, the Republican nominee, our California friend, has been playing on the outskirts with our enemies and our friends both, he has been doing it through rather subterranean sources here. And he has been saying to the allies that you're gonna get sold out. You better not give away your liberty just a few hours before I can preserve it for you. Mrs. Chennault is contacting their ambassador. Now this is not guess work. Mrs. Chennault, she's young and attractive, she's a pretty good looking girl. And she's around town and she's warning them not to get pulled in on this Johnson move.

Johnson quickly ordered the FBI to wiretap the Nixon

campaign. He learned of Nixon's use of Anna Chennault as a liaison between South Vietnam's ambassador to the US, Bui Diem, and himself. Through Chennault, Nixon facilitated Nguyên Văn Thiêu's continued boycott of the Paris peace talks. Johnson studied the secret FBI cables and began working phones to thwart the Nixon campaign's strategies. He contacted senate republican leader Everett Dirksen about the acts of treason.

LBJ: I want to talk to you as a friend, and very confidentially, because I think that we're skirting on dangerous ground. I thought I ought to give you the facts, and you ought to pass them on if you choose. If you don't, why, then I will later.

Dirksen: Yeah.

LBJ: We have, on October the 13th, an agreement with Thiêu and Ky (Thiêu's vice president), considering the bombing halt.

Dirksen: Yeah.

LBJ: At that time, President Thiêu stressed, quote 'there must not be a long delay.'

Dirksen: Yeah.

LBJ: That is, a delay between the halt and the conference.

Dirksen: Yeah.

LBJ: On October 15, Thiêu agreed to a proposal that we worked out of 36 hours.

Dirksen: Yeah.

LBJ: "On October 23, after the North Vietnamese demanded two or three weeks, Thiêu reluctantly agreed to three days delay. On October 28, we agreed on the joint announcement.

Dirksen: Yeah.

LBJ: Bunker (Ellsworth) and [Creighton] Abrams (commander of military operations, 1968-1972) reached an explicit agreement with Thiêu that the gap between the bombing and the talks would be two or three days, with three days the outer limit. Both Thiêu and Ky stressed on us the importance of a minimum delay.

Dirksen: Yeah.

LBJ: Then we got some of our friends involved. Some of it's your old China crowd...

Dirksen: Yeah.

LBJ: And… here's the latest information we got: the agent says that she's—they've just talked to the boss (Nixon) in New Mexico, and that he says that you must hold out, that... Just hold on until after the election. Now we know what Thiêu is saying to 'em out there. We're pretty well informed on both ends.

Dirksen: Yeah.

LBJ: Now Nixon's man traveling with him today, said quote 'He did not understand that Thiêu was not aboard. Did you see that?

Dirksen: No, I didn't. Who was that?'

LBJ: We don't know... no idea. He speaks through these unknown people. Now, we told Nixon as we told Thiêu... now, let me get the transcript. While this was going on, we went out to Thiêu and talked to him, and all of our allied countries, and they all tentatively agreed. Now.

On November 2, three days prior to the election, Johnson placed a phone call to Republican Senate Minority Leader Everett Dirksen demanding he take necessary action. He voiced his concern to Dirksen, suggesting that he might go public with the information. Dirksen agreed with the president that Nixon's acts were treason. However they both felt the American people would be shocked if they knew a major candidate was playing political games with the course of a war.

Fearing the president could go public with his knowledge of the campaign's acts of conspiracy, Nixon contacted Johnson directly the afternoon of November 3. He explained his take on events and that he'd read the report from Everett Dirksen and went on the Sunday morning news show *Meet the Press.* Nixon assured Johnson total cooperation before the election and, in the event that he was elected, after the election. He made his interest in seeing Saigon come to the peace talks clear.

The president proceeded with caution, being careful not to set Nixon on the defensive. He told him, "Dick… that is what's taking place. I just wanted you to know." It was an estranged alliance, and each man had a motive for allowing such conspiracy. A second reason Johnson did not go public with the information—even though doing so could have cost Nixon the election—was that by revealing the information Johnson revealed the illegal way it was acquired.[21]

Beverly Deepe, a correspondent for the *Christian Science Monitor,* was stationed in Saigon. She had been informed by South Vietnamese sources about the Nixon campaign's requests for Thiêu to prolong the peace talks. Deepe sent in a draft of the story she'd written to her magazine:

> "Purported political encouragement from the Richard Nixon camp was a significant factor in the last-minute decision of President Thiêu's refusal to send a delegation to the Paris peace talks—at least until the American presidential election is over."

Facts were checked, and a journalist (Saville Davis) from the *Monitor's* Washington office, confirmed the story with South Vietnamese Ambassador Bui Diem. The article was then vetted by the White house.

The president met with advisors on what to do. Secretary of State Dean Rusk, Defense Secretary Clark Clifford (Robert McNamara had resigned in February), and Walt Rowstow all favored silence on the matter. Clifford thought the story had many shocking elements. He knew that the image of the US government was at stake. It was felt that the story was so inflammatory that disclosing it, and having Nixon elected, was too much for America to handle. The defense secretary said such information was bound to put the nation into such massive speculation about Nixon's administration that it was unfavorable to America's interests. They reasoned that the majority of Americans were generally satisfied with the performance of government. The plot to sabotage the election was never revealed. Arguably, because of the preferred silence on treason, the war continued for five years and cost billions of dollars and more than fifteen thousand American lives.

Ψ

The two months of campaigning that preceded the general election were marred by short funding for Humphrey. He trailed Nixon, and donations were scarce. In September Johnson persuaded fellow Texas Democrats to support his vice president and finally gave Humphrey his own endorsement later that fall in a radio address. On the campaign trail Humphrey attacked Nixon, saying he was a hawk who had said in 1954 that he wanted to go to war with Vietnam. Nixon's running mate, Spiro Agnew, claimed that Humphrey was too soft on Communism, inflation and law and order. The vice president had his running mate, Senator Edmund Muskie (D-ME), retaliate. The two-term senator was known to be a skilled campaigner and for his ability to quell hostile anti-war protesters, occasionally inviting them to join him on stage. He faulted Nixon and Agnew for ignoring issues such as urban renewal, housing and federal aid for education.

In a September Gallup poll the Republican presidential candidate retained a lead of fifteen points—44 percent to 29. At the end of September, Lawrence O'Brien (Democratic National Committee chairman) advised that Humphrey break from the

Johnson administration and in a televised speech from Salt Lake City the vice president promised to end the North Vietnam bombing if elected. He claimed that his call for a ceasefire to be "an acceptable risk for peace."[23]

Days before the election Humphrey secured the endorsement of Eugene McCarthy. The ceasefire and peace talks appeared to push him closer to a win, closing Nixon's eighteen point lead to two by the end of October. The Paris peace talks were now being influenced by the Soviet Union. They sought to convince North Vietnam to be soft on the negotiations in order to prevent a Nixon win. On November 4, the evening before election day, each candidate hosted a televised forum. Nixon knew that "tons of supplies"[24] were being channeled into North Vietnam along the Ho Chi Minh Trail. His strategy was to dull the momentum Humphrey had gained by the bombing halt.

1968 General Election

Presidential Candidate/Party	Home State	Popular Vote	% Electoral Votes
Richard M Nixon R	NY	31,783,783	43.4
Hubert H Humphrey D	MN	31,271,839	42.7
George C Wallace IN	AL	9,901,118	13.5

Vice Presidential Candidate/Party	Home State	Electoral Votes
Spiro T Agnew R	MD	301
Edmund S Muskie D	ME	191
Curtis E LeMay IN	CA	46

The term "realigning election" has been used to describe the 1968 presidential election. It forever upset the New Deal coalition as it refers to the alignment of interest groups. The New Deal coalition is the voting blocs that supported Roosevelt's New Deal. It was the people who voted Democratic from 1932 to the late 1960s. In that time frame, the Democrats had won seven out of the nine presidential elections.

Ψ

When Richard Milhous Nixon was sworn in as our 37th president I was just shy of five years old. In a few ways, the war's various proliferations reflected in my youth. Ironies can get tempestuous. As I look at black and white photographs from 1969, I stand in a crew cut with a hesitant smile on my face. I wonder if I felt the loss of everything for which my parents—and all those I'd come to know—had worked so hard. I wonder if my expression looks hesitant because so much hopelessness, anger and conviction existed. The Vietnam War danced on. Our new Republican president, whom I was taught to jeer, made sure of that. I danced on in hopscotches. Our government tread on an ever-thinning wire. The country was set on a swivel in a game of popularity until the beans fell with Saigon. My perennial junctures in life coincided with those casual paces the war took forward. I was brought up on it. It brought me up in a diametrically opposed world. The opportunities the war opened for long-term societal change nurtured me. On February 1, 1971, the American military paused to look at itself, to see how unaware of its purpose it had become. That day I turned six years old in a comatose state. I had been adopted by a couple who stood out to oppose an illegal war. When I was coming into this world the first major offensive action by the US against North Vietnam was beginning. The plans for Operation Rolling Thunder were approved February 13, 1965. Four years later, before the chair in the Oval Office—or the vetted parallels on Vietnam's grid—could cool, Nixon widened the war.

Ψ

Nixon vowed to end the war on his own terms—with honor for America. Later that winter, the Viet Cong attacked target areas of South Vietnam, laying ground work for what eventually led to the fall of Saigon. In response to attacks on the South, Nixon resumed bombing North Vietnam. He insisted significant US forces be kept in South Vietnam indefinitely. He stated many of his intentions, contrary to what public image was conveyed, privately to Morton Halperin. Halperin had worked under Johnson as an advisor and was considered an expert on foreign policy. Nixon told Mort frequently that he was "prepared to carry out the full-scale…" and attack North Vietnam much harder than Johnson ever did. He cited his predecessor's reticence in the war. If the North Vietnamese Army (NVA) did not relent he wanted to mine North Vietnam's harbors and blockade them. Nixon pledged to bomb populations and use nuclear weapons if necessary.

The events from 1969 to 1975 were known as the "bitter end of the war." Nixon saw it as a challenge. Johnson had not done enough. He had not invested enough in 'protecting' South Vietnam. Nixon thought he could and should do better to repel the North Vietnamese. He pledged to "…carry out, if necessary, heavier destruction than the North has ever actually experienced before. And I'll demonstrate that meanwhile by expanding the war in ways that Lyndon Johnson didn't dare."[25]

Johnson had halted the bombing only above the twentieth parallel when he withdrew as an incumbent presidential candidate. Serious negotiations with Hanoi were sought, giving middle-America a sense that they were seeing a turning point in the war. From March 1968 until Nixon's invasion of Cambodia in April 1970, the war in Vietnam shrunk from mainstream American political debate. A study headed by Morton Halperin concluded that, with the cessation of all North Vietnam bombing after November 1968 and the negotiation with Hanoi, Johnson had "for a time removed the issue of Vietnam from domestic political contention."

That brief pax Vietnam misled a majority of Americans. It had given them a false sense of security—once again—that peace was imminent. Vietnam was somewhat of a lesser issue. With the exception of the tumultuous Chicago convention in August that year, Johnson withdrew from the presidential race during a period of relative peace.

Less than a week after the election, accusations and anticipations of Nixon's agenda circled the Oval Office. Henry Kissinger, in his low, Germanic accent reiterated, "Richard Nixon is not fit to be president."[26]

In March of 1969 he ordered US troops for offensive action on the Demilitarized Zone (DMZ). The targets now were in Laos and Cambodia. Nixon's offensive strikes that spring—dubbed Operation Menu—showered Cambodia with bombs dropped from B-52s. His operation usurped his predecessor's in gross tonnage of bombs. The plan was to cut key North Vietnamese supply sanctuaries stationed along the Vietnamese border. No Republican administration is ever satisfied with what a Democratic administration did—even if it's the aggressiveness taken to ensure an honorable ending to a war. America must not look weak. The incoming administration must up the ante, until hawkish talons can silence birds of a feather, to more soundly mute the strangled songs of doves.

Chapter Nine

The War Machine

Popularity contests never turn out well in the "land of the free and the home of the brave." Who is brave and who is free? More importantly, who is free to be brave and brave enough to be free? Pluralities, the minority of minions; the opinionated, mutinous Democrats I watched being formed, comprised the brave. I saw the players. I spent the more enlightening years of my boyhood around people who did give "democracy its day in court." But also, located far away from the DFL, WILPF and the pragmatic sounds of politics that bounced from our rambler's walls every day, there existed young men and women whose hair trigger response, when faced with armed National Guardsmen, chose to poke flowers into the threatening gun barrels. I learned that it was brave *not* to stand up and pull the trigger simply because your government wanted you to fight their unconstitutional and immoral war. Thousands of young men went to jail for refusing to go to Vietnam. They stood for their principles; they stood for the morality our involvement in Vietnam lacked.

When Nixon took office in 1969 draft-age men were returning from the Peace Corps. In 1960 he said that Kennedy's program was a "haven for draft dodgers."[1] Young people publicly burned draft cards. They booked flights to Canada or feigned maladies at induction physicals. College enrollment skyrocketed. Those who chose to remain in America spoke out against the war. Many who served and returned also spoke out against the war. Legal cases involving the Selective Service were particularly high in Minnesota.

Ψ

The earliest form of organized military service began in Salem, Massachusetts. Governor John Winthrop mandated that able-bodied white males between age sixteen and sixty possess firearms. The 1636 order obligated them to defend their community and participate in weekly drills and nightly guard details.

Objection to war and the resistance to conscripted service in America has a long history. The Enrollment Act, or Civil War Military Draft Act, was enacted in March of 1863 to provide fresh troops for the Union Army. It called for males age twenty to forty-five including immigrants who intended to become citizens. Objection to the enforcement of the act was common and even incited a riot in New York during the summer of 1863. Commutation was a policy by which a man could pay $300 to be relieved from conscripted service in the military. One could either buy his way out or find a substitute to fight in his stead. Future president Grover Cleveland, then working as an assistant district attorney in New York, paid a thirty-two-year-old Polish immigrant $150 to serve in his place. Beginning in 1861 the Confederacy enacted a number of conscription laws in order to build its army. In October of 1862, after much lobbying, the Confederate Congress passed what was known as the "twenty Negro law." The law granted exemption from service to an owner or one overseer of twenty able-bodied slaves.

Following the French Revolution, national military conscription became common in Europe and in the latter part of the nineteenth century; the absence of compulsory service in the military was an attraction for immigrants to America. Prior to our entry into the First World War, thousands of immigrants came to America fleeing conscription. When the US declared war on Germany in April 1917, President Woodrow Wilson signed a Selective Service Act authorizing the federal government to build a national army for our entry into WWI. It was the first war to use classification for conscripted service:

Classifications & Categories for Military Service (May 1917-July 1919)

- I **Eligible and liable for service**—unmarried registrants with no dependents or married registrants with an independent spouse and/or one or more dependent children over 16 with sufficient income if drafted.
- II **Temporarily deferred, but available for service**—married registrants with dependent spouse and/or dependent children under sixteen with sufficient income if drafted.
- III **Exempted, but available for service**—local officials, registrants who provide the sole income to dependent parents and/or dependent siblings under sixteen, or registrants employed in agriculture or vocation necessary to war effort.
- IV **Exempted due to extreme hardship**—registrants with a deceased spouse who provide the sole income for dependent children under sixteen, married registrants with a dependent spouse and/or dependent children with inadequate income if drafted, or registrants of deceased parents who provide the sole income to siblings under sixteen.
- V **Ineligible for service**—state or federal officials, members of the clergy, or registrants found to be medically disabled or morally unfit for duty.

Objectors to the Second World War studied writings of the Fellowship of Reconciliation (FOR), the oldest interfaith peace organization in the United States, and the War Resister's League, the United States' oldest secular pacifist organization. Following WWII there was an overflow of young men. They were eligible, and many voluntarily enlisted to serve their country. During WWII the oldest available men were the first to be drafted. In 1961, when voluntary service began to subside, President Kennedy thought that by revising the selection process, he could improve the system. Married men went to the bottom of the selection, and students were routinely granted deferment. During this time other policies were implemented and plugged by army recruitment. Social rehabilitation and the war on poverty were promoted with the escalating conflict in Southeast Asia.

"Then came the buildup in Vietnam, and I watched the program broken and eviscerated as if it were some idle political plaything of a society gone mad on war." - Martin Luther King, Jr., 1968

In 1951 the Universal and Military Training Act had made it compulsory to register for the draft at eighteen. Men were eligible to serve from age eighteen and a half to twenty-six. The government began to classify those registered. Men were classified according to their mental and physical ability to serve. Those who went to war now were typically younger than their predecessors. From 1958 to 1964, the typical draft age was nineteen to twenty-four. In the course of those six years the number of draftees grew from eight million to twelve million. There were also pacifists, conscientious objectors, and draft resisters. In many cases, they were in school or otherwise were not required to serve at the time they were called. The students were given deferments; they showed up at the induction center, took the physical exam and were classified 1-S. The resisters without deferments were classified 1-A and were able to serve when they were called. Others held on to their religious principles. They sought conscientious objector, or CO, status. They were either classified 1-A-O, available for noncombatant military service, or 1-O, available for civilian work that contributed to the maintenance of national health or safety.

In 1967 an attempt was made to reform draft laws. President Johnson appointed The Marshall Commission to make recommendations. The commission's report, *Equity: Who Should Serve When Not All Serve*, made many amendments to the draft system. One was an arbitrary selection process to take the place of the then-existing order-of-call regulations. Congress did not approve any of the amendments. Instead, the law it did pass, the Military Selective Service Act of 1967, included an all-encompassing deferment for undergraduates until they finished school. It also called for the drafting of the youngest men first. The law also mandated the development of a lottery system.

Opposition to the draft increased, and the Department of Justice indicted resisters in record numbers. By 1969, four thousand resistance cases had been through the courts. In Minnesota, Judge Miles Lord presided over many of the Selective Service cases. In a March 1968 case, two defendants were brought before him for arraignment. Bail was set at $3,000 apiece. One defendant's counsel made a motion to reduce his client's bail to $1,500. Lord obliged but refused to release the accused to his attorney. The judge was firm and fair, but idealistic. A memorandum quoted the judge:

> "After they have a few days in jail and get an idea of what the regimentation is there and how the freedoms for which they fight and protest will be deprived of them for two years, they might more seriously consider the course they are taking."[2]

In reducing the dissenter's bail, Lord was quoted as saying "(I hope) if he has friends and relatives they won't make bail for him."[3] The following day the *Minneapolis Star* ran two letters to the editor on the subject. One rose to the judge's defense, claiming "not (to) threaten these young men with imprisonment to deter them from exercising their rights." The other condemned Lord, suggesting that "a judge who is so certain that these men will be convicted that he recommends a preview of jail for them should not be trying this case."[4] Days later, the honorable Judge Miles Lord bowed out of the case.

By 1972, Selective Service indictments accounted for more than half of the federal criminal cases in Minnesota. Some of those involved Jehovah's Witnesses and Quakers who were denied conscientious objector status and refused induction. Lord found many of the defendants that appeared before him guilty, however only a small number were sent to prison. Typically he sentenced the accused resister to twenty-four months on probation during which they performed work similar to what conscientious objectors did. This work usually consisted of soil conservation or forestry. A bumper sticker put out by a coalition called "GI free" read:

Send a Congressman to
Vietnam – not me!
National GI week October 21-27

Never before had the resisters of a war been as well-defined and organized. Never before had the constitution's system of checks and balances been so blatantly disregarded. Congress has the power to declare war. The president has the authority to send and command ground troops. Many opposed to the war simply ignored their induction notices based on prior disagreements with America's policies in Indochina. Others based their rejection of the government on how the draft disproportionately selected African-Americans.

Civilian Public Service
American Friends
Service Committee

"TO SUBSTITUTE ORDER
FOR CHAOS AND CREATION
FOR DESTRUCTION"

25 Twenty five cents —25

(A 1941 sticker sums up the sentiments of the American Friends Service Committee.)

Over half of the requests for CO status during the Vietnam War were from Jehovah's Witnesses. From 1960 to 1975, approximately 170,000 men received CO deferments from service in Southeast Asia. In WWII there were 72,354 applications for CO status beginning with the US declaration of war (December 8, 1941) through victory in Japan (September 2, 1945). Of those requesting CO deferments during the Vietnam War, 25,000 consented to serve in positions in the army that did not require them to breach their ethics; another 27,000 failed the physical exam. Ultimately, 6,086 COs went to prison for failing to comply with the Selective Service. An additional 12,000 of those seeking CO status agreed to Civilian Public Service (CPS). Under the direction of civilian authorities, they did work designated to be of "national importance." There were CPS camps, most of which were run by groups like the Mennonites, Quakers and Brethren.

There were those, such as Muhammad Ali, who insisted the conflict had no claim on them. Ali—then Cassius Clay—failed tests to qualify for service in 1964. In November 1965, the standards for entry into the military service were lowered. Ali's status was changed to 1-A the following February. The heavyweight boxer publicly stated that he was a conscientious objector, claiming "War is against the teachings of the Holy Qur'an. I'm not trying to dodge the draft. We are not supposed to take part in no wars unless declared by Allah or The Messenger. We don't take part in Christian wars or wars of any unbelievers." His refusal to be drafted was based on Islamic principles rather than indifference to the war. "I ain't got no quarrel with the Viet Cong. …They never called me nigger."[5] Ali spoke out on civil rights and the war. Such activism was unprecedented for a boxer and resonated with people.

Ψ

Throughout 1967, the effectiveness of the bombing was continually questioned in American intelligence reports. In September it was reported through intelligence that "The NV (North Vietnam) transport system has emerged from more than thirty months of bombing with greater capacity and flexibility than it had when the operation began."[6] Secretary of State Dean Rusk questioned why the North Vietnamese wanted the bombing stopped if it was not having a great effect. National Security advisor Walter Rostow pointed out that in fact the bombing had, by diverting workers to other jobs, cut industrial and agricultural production in the North. He warned that if the bombing was stopped, North Vietnam could repair its economy and increase its intrusion into South Vietnam.

Records from an October 3, 1967 meeting with Secretary of State Rusk report of his meeting with the United Nations General Assembly. Rusk claimed he had been to many meetings with various bilateral groups, and no one was able predict the effects of ending Operation Rolling Thunder. Russian foreign minister Andrei Gromyko reported that the Soviets had abandoned the idea of influencing Hanoi. Both sides were tired and frustrated, although neither wanted to admit it.

Prior to being Richard Nixon's national security advisor, Harvard professor Henry Kissinger worked as a consultant on foreign policy to the White House and the State Department. In August of 1965 he was asked by his friend Henry Cabot Lodge, Jr. (ambassador to Saigon) to visit Vietnam as his consultant. Kissinger made a total of three trips to Vietnam, the last in October of 1966. Increasingly, the tours convinced Kissinger that any military victory would be meaningless "…unless they (the North Vietnamese) brought about a political reality that could survive our ultimate withdrawal."[7]

A massive anti-war rally was planned for the weekend of October 21-22, 1967. The president was determined not to be influenced by the rally. He instructed Defense Secretary McNamara to begin plans to defend the White House, Pentagon and Capitol. Deputy Attorney General Warren Christopher was appointed to head an interdepartmental task force, designed specifically to thwart the demonstration. McNamara reported that Washington DC police and National Guard troops were trained to handle the demonstrators. The possible arrest of thousands was anticipated as well as where to jail them "if it was justified."[8]

In February 1966, a private meeting took place in a Honolulu hotel room. Among those present were journalists, other correspondents and the secretary of defense. Robert McNamara seized the semi-private opportunity to state his belief that no amount of bombing could end the war. By August 1967, McNamara had testified in hearings concerning Operation Rolling Thunder at the Senate's Preparedness Investigative Subcommittee. The subcommittee was chaired by Senator John C. Stennis, D-Miss., and consisted of people who shared equally hawkish sensibilities. Weary of war, tired of defending a losing fight, the defense secretary again stated his belief: he offered that no amount of bombing could succeed in ending the war "short, that is, of the total annihilation of North Vietnam and its people."[9]

In the months that followed McNamara's summation, attitudes concerning the war morale in the White House changed. He was burned out, and the confidence he had in the war that led him in orchestrating it with precise calculations was gone. The war had taken its toll on him, and he frequently sought refuge in his private Pentagon office. Early in November, in a memorandum to the president, McNamara recommended freezing troop levels, halting the bombing of North Vietnam and handing ground fighting over to the South Vietnamese army. Johnson rejected all of the defense secretary's recommendations. To the president, McNamara's ideas implied that all the US strategy maintained thus far had failed. The dismissal of his memo prompted McNamara to hand in his resignation at the end of the month. He left office at the end of February the following year. The president had announced Clark Clifford as McNamara's successor earlier in January. Clifford was said to be more of a hawk than a dove. He stated that unlike his predecessor, he was "not conscious of falling under any of those ornithological divisions."

Johnson also questioned his own longevity. "Our people will not hold out four more years," he said, and vowed to "work my guts out" in the remaining months of his term. If Johnson began a second full term he'd be sixty-five by the time he completed it. He questioned his ability to deal with "four more year of this."[10] The president weighed his options. He considered the effect announcing his intent not to run for another term could have. He considered the timing of such an announcement. Robert McNamara confessed he had no idea of how such an announcement might affect the morale of the troops or perceptions of the government in Hanoi. The defense secretary was sure of one thing though: if Johnson stepped out of the running, any negotiations with Hanoi had to wait until after the 1968 election.

Ψ

I walked to the TV to turn the dial of our black and white set. I turned it fast with childish arbitration. I hoped that I discovered *Gilligan's Island* before anything concerning the war caught my eye. War, on a scale appropriate for its destructive power, had made its television debut. The news broadcasts influenced how most of America understood the war. They provided an appreciation for the mass destruction and civilian casualties like no war before had. When the Second Indochina war began, US journalists supported our efforts and reported on them extensively. Live images of the dying, the devastation and looks of hopeless bewilderment on nineteen-year-old faces played in living rooms across America every night.

Blades of Chinook choppers spun American sensibility. Pensive young soldiers crouched awkwardly inside of them, clutching bayonets timidly for security. The choppers matted grass and the jungle foliage we later burned. Images of medics—one of whom was the son of Marie, the woman who read to me in the hospital—consoling their peers, assuring them that they'll be all right, are hard to obscure.

The reports never included any background on Vietnam's long history of suppression by foreign rule. Journalistic integrity faced a major threat. In 1967, defense secretary Robert McNamara delivered news of the war to journalists at the Pentagon. He answered their questions with a kind of optimism that was often misleading. Even the North Vietnamese press made efforts to sway world opinion against the war. By 1968, our government could not rely on media to sell its war anymore. In February that year, following the CBS documentary "Report from Vietnam," Walter Cronkite read an editorial in which he declared the war a stalemate. Rumors later surfaced that, upon hearing the editorial, President Johnson lamented that if he'd lost Cronkite, he'd lost Middle America.

Chapter Ten

Motives & Strategies

"Your mother worked much harder than I did."[1] My dad's work in politics utilized, for the most part, skills learned as a public speaker and educator. He chaired caucuses and was elected to be a delegate to county and state conventions. He enjoyed the challenge, the people he met and what was learned. I never saw my mom, though, as a hard player of politics. She was more grassroots in her approach. To her it was simply a necessary means to an end. They had an equal commitment to a goal, but it was approached differently.

Richfield resident Edward Donahue, president of the Twin Cities Lithographer's Union, came to our house for meetings of McCarthy delegates. As a union leader, his actions were likely questioned or even resented by union members. The smaller labor unions generally disliked Senator McCarthy and tended to support Humphrey-Johnson. Toward the close of a DFL meeting my mom questioned Donahue's reputation as a union president after he was so vocal about his support of McCarthy. He replied, "Like hell I can't."[2] (speak about McCarthy). He knew the balancing point between labor and politics and how to keep the lithographers and DFL cronies in tow. Later, in the 1970s, Ed and his wife moved from Richfield. They still visited sometimes, often unannounced, from

Washington, DC. He parked a recreational vehicle in the turn-around of our driveway. He always had a little motorcycle strapped on the back of the RV. His wife, a woman he called Bert, had little interest in politics. She read and smoked cigarettes, meandering from room to room in our house when Ed went off on his motorcycle to visit friends and political contacts around Richfield. I guess opposites do attract.

The Minneapolis-based Honeywell Corporation had the largest military contract in the country during the Vietnam War. Its cluster bombs carpeted Southeast Asia, indiscriminately killing military personal and civilians. Marv Davidov was a political activist who carried around a softball-sized prototype of a cluster bomb in a knapsack for display. Davidov's Honeywell Project came from an idea he got from an article by Staughton Lynd, a Quaker and conscientious objector. Lynd's article suggested anti-war activists show their opposition by bringing the protests to corporations that were profiting from the war. Davidov and other activists in Minnesota started ferreting out local corporations with ties to the military. His project was formed to challenge the corporation's participation in the Vietnam War and its military contracts in general. The program organized cultural and educational events. Often these were combined with large demonstrations outside Honeywell's headquarters in South Minneapolis. Some of their slogans and demands were:

- Peace conversion without loss of jobs
- No components for nuclear weapons
- No cluster bombs or other conventional weapons
- Worker and community control over Honeywell and the nation's corporation

Davidov led the protests at Honeywell in the late 60s and early 70s, one in which my mom marched.

Around the time of the protests my dad was moonlighting as an independent consultant for Honeywell. The company hired him to work with their ordnance division. He consulted for them to help them work more creatively. He says he felt some dissonance for doing something that was helping a major military supplier. I don't know how he rationalized working for Honeywell, or if he even attempted to do so. However, many regular employees of Honeywell *did* feel a need to rationalize what they did. It was a coveted company to work for, and no one left due to a conflict of ethics. A transfer could be obtained within the company. If one was working in a department whose end product was a cluster bomb, they could request to work in a department that made, for example, thermostats. No ill-will was bore them, and personal beliefs and opinions were respected.

A 1974 Dump the war Rally in Bloomington, MN
(from left: Al Lowenstein, Mom, John Helmberger,
and congressman Donald Reigel.
Photo courtesy of the *Richfield Sun*)

I heard my mom referred to as a muckraker a handful of times growing up. She first heard the term in reference to her while I was attending high school. Originally, the label was used in referring to journalists. It gained popularity in the early 1900s in America's *Progressive Era,* which ran from the 1890s to the 1920s. Muckrakers were known for exposing the injustices of society. For the most part, the injustices my mom exposed had a limited audience. Outside of the political arena, as a mother raising impressionable children, her muckraking had benign purposes.

Ψ

"The consumer boycott is the only open door in the dark corridor of nothingness down which farm workers have had to walk for many years. It is a gate of hope through which they expect to find the sunlight of a better life for themselves and their families." - Cesar Chavez

The Great Depression had left thousands unemployed, and one effect was that Caucasian Americans took jobs that were previously filled by migrant farm workers. In California this left many Mexicans and Filipinos out of work. They did anything for work and, as Steinbeck describes in the 1939 novel *The Grapes of Wrath,* conditions were far from desirable for farm workers. The unsanitary conditions and paltry wages sparked fierce debate between worker and employer. The Great Depression, and its implications for the farm worker, set the stage for fifty years of wage strikes, boycotts and labor disputes.

In 1964 Cesar Chavez and Deloris Huerta formed The United Farm Worker's Association (UFWA). To bolster support for the union, Chavez organized a march from Delano to Sacramento (340 miles). Chavez and his followers gained national attention. Still, efforts to get the grape producers to the bargaining table fell short. The UFWA tried a new tactic. From 1966 to 1970 the United Farm Worker's Organizing Committee led a boycott of all table grapes. It received worldwide support and became the most successful boycott in American history.

DON'T BUY SUPPORT
NON-GRAPES Farm-workers
UFWAFL-CIO

My mom wore a UFWA button on the lapel of her tan, leather overcoat. I was indifferent to having grapes. Susan, though, had a fondness for them. She asked my mom to buy them. My mom bought them for her until she heard about the boycott. After more than five years of marches, protests and community organization, California passed a law. In 1975 secret balloting was allowed in union representation elections for farm workers. The Delano boycott was the most successful in history.

Ψ

Blackened clumps of snow fell from the bumpers of parked cars. They dropped with a conspicuous *slushhhh* in the solitude of the garage. My pupils darted back and forth (nystagmus), finally focusing on salt stains that sprawled on the garage floor. They conspired in the heat to lead me like they were bloated bread crumbs. Fluorescent lights haloed the cars as we walked in their shadows. My dad parked his Opel in the underground heated garage of an office building on 74th and Lyndale. For three or four years after the car accident, my parents' political involvement was much less intense. I was high maintenance. During the summer of 1971, my dad and I walked daily, either in Richfield or at our cabin up north. He palmed a silver counter on our walks and tallied my steps on scratch pads. Every four hundred steps I made without falling earned a reward. Friends looked at me from their bikes, some empathetic of where I was and cheering for where I had to go, others still showing off what they could still do. I slowly made my way toward a neighbor's house at the end of Aldrich Avenue on top of a small hill. I concentrated, but still I saw them out of the corner of my eye. Their voices battled for me to hear them. Their presence only reminded me I'd never coast down the Oak Grove hill on my blue and white bike.

At the top of the hill lived a lady who was never known to be overly generous. When I reached her house, though, she almost always offered me an ice cream cone. When my dad and I walked at our cabin it was usually the half-mile down to the general store. The Iron Rangers in the store, the anglers and curmudgeons, probably wanted to talk politics. They'd have given my dad a good, amenable talk. He did not indulge them though. The cabin was our retreat, and politics and pressures of the university were left in the cities.

After about two and a half seasons at Michael Dowling School on the Mississippi's west bank, I went back to Richfield Schools in a transition program called *mainstreaming.* A doctor who I still saw at the university's rehabilitation department said "mainstreaming is okay as long as you don't drown." I walked with wooden crutches in a wide ataxic gait. They had canvas cuffs that circled just above my elbows. I went back to Central Elementary in the fall of 1974. The previous year a new Rehabilitation Act replaced the Vocational Rehabilitation Act. It extended the authorization of grants to states for vocational rehabilitation services. The legislation eventually changed the way needs were accommodated for students whose needs went outside the normal. In the fall of 1973 the bill was signed into law by President Nixon—the same man who had succeeded in protracting a war.

My sister always held the door for me. Teacher's said, "Oh, I had your sister in my class." Following her made assimilating to a hostile environment a little easier. For what it was worth, I knew my name had some credibility, with the teachers anyway. At the end of the year Susan left for the junior high school. I felt alone, kind of like a fish out of an acclimated stream that suddenly finds itself in a main stream. She had been an exemplary student and put the Amram name in the best light. The bar was set high for me to reach. I don't think I ever consciously tried that hard to touch it. As much as I wanted to rebel in school against bullies—finally realizing that was not going to happen—I noticed a subconscious need to compromise and meet that bar half way. I was a charming kid (as a medical record reported) and that helped. Still, that first year, I was targeted for being physically different—as well as a couple of other things.

Cultural diversity was always nurtured and encouraged in our house. It found its way to our table each spring at Passover. One or two families were always invited to our Seder. As Reform Jews, we made our own traditions. My dad always led the Seder, delegating readings from the Haggadah (Hebrew book that tells of the Exodus) to us and our guests. We read from right to left, and my dad leaned on a pillow. He did this to symbolize how the pharaohs and emperors ate while their slaves usually squatted (however, I doubt that we made our guests squat). Our Seder was much abridged and left time for reading individual pieces at the Seder. It was not mandatory, but appreciated. Guests brought poems, news clipping, songs or book passages. All told something of themselves, their culture, their religion and how they saw the centuries-old Jewish tradition. Many Seders, as a kid, I read from Martin Luther King's "I Have a Dream" speech. The poignant parts from the speech were paraphrased for me:

"I have a dream today.

Someday little black boys and little black girls will join hands with little white boys and little white girls and walk together as sisters and brothers.

I have a dream today.

Someday all God's children will join hands.

Together they will sing the old Negro song, 'free at last, free at last. Thank God almighty, we are free at last.'"[3]

I was encouraged to read it each year. My words wobbled meekly across the table, desperately seeking some semblance of the power with which they were first spoken. The script was creased in the pages of my Haggadah, stained with grape juice. Freedom is a theme of Passover celebrations. Seder means order, and it ritualistically tells of the story of the Exodus from Egypt. The ten plagues that God rained on Egypt and Moses parting the Red Sea are faith-based. Slavery and human oppression are all too real. What abolishes them, or at least subdues them, through doctrine or alleged miracles, is the part where faith is imperative. Whether or not one chooses to believe in the divine power of Moses and his staff to part the Red Sea and lead the Israelites out of bondage is irrelevant. The relevant moral is that the stories have given Jews hope for centuries, at times literally keeping them alive.

We searched for the Afikoman (matzo).[4] Susan and I kept close watch on the pillow on which my dad leaned. He always wrapped one matzo half in a cloth napkin and tucked it safely behind the pillow. At some point in the Seder it always disappeared! It was dessert, and the rules said we needed it to complete the meal. Whoever found it received a small prize. We nibbled at it as we finished telling the story of Exodus. Our Reform Seders were long, and when I looked at a clock I realized at least four hours had elapsed. At some point toward the end of the Seder the door is opened for Elijah. The rush of the cold night air was always a jolt. The idea was that food and drink were offered to the poor and downtrodden. I don't remember any homeless ever coming to our door. I do recall the silver goblet filled with wine. In spite of our close surveillance, it always appeared to be half empty when the door was closed.

The final sentiment of Passover was always the same. We vowed to never stop fighting, protesting or vehemently calling for a world that is free of tyranny. It never is. At best it gets better, and it gets worse—at least enough to give some reason to keep on battling injustices. While I sat at those Seders, a form of tyranny was being inflicted upon the South Vietnamese. It was going on in America. It was happening in the city streets and in induction centers across the nation.

"May the light of freedom penetrate into all corners of the world and lift the darkness of tyranny until tyranny is no more, so that all men may be free."[5] It was never trite or hyperbolic. The words that ended our Seder each year were exercised every day.

Ψ

Radical woman's liberation took its roots in the United States in the late 1960s. Robin Morgan led groups like New York Radical Women (NYRW). She was influenced by the Yippies who aimed to shock and offend mainstream America. In 1969 WITCH (Woman's International Terrorist Conspiracy from Hell) was formed as NYRW became divided. They disagreed mainly on the role consciousness raising—bringing mainstream attention to a cause—had in the woman's movement. Consciousness raising (CR) separated into a group referred to as "Redstockings." Women who advocated more political action and social autonomy stayed with WITCH. The radical feminists took direct action. They protested in 1968, for example, at the Miss America Pageant by throwing high heels as well as bras into garbage cans.

Redstockings

I never saw feminism displayed quite that brazenly. However, the idea that women should be equal to men in every aspect of life was certainly encouraged. Most mothers on Aldrich Avenue waited complacently for their husbands to come home and crack a beer as dinner was made for them in a clean house. In our house, gender roles were never assigned or assumed—never! Steps were taken to ensure we grew up knowing a woman could do a man's job and vice versa. If I wanted to play with a doll rather than a truck (I did both), nothing was said. My sister was never given a Barbie doll. My mom thought the doll's image was of a woman whose only contributions to society were blonde hair and a perfect figure.

My mom was in her late thirties and had dealt with gender inequalities longer than many of the women on our block.

As I mentioned earlier, her salary as a social worker was not acknowledged when she and my dad applied for a housing loan in 1959. She'd come from New York already progressively minded. I always thought a measured dose of Bronx chutzpah figured into her politics. An article in the *Richfield Sun,* April 23, 1970, featured a dialogue with my mom and three other women, all involved in politics to varying degrees. The article focused on a woman's role in the house and in political circles. Men were learning that they could take part in household roles without compromising their masculinity. My mom stated that "Fred will babysit, but he won't do the dishes."[6] She and two other women on the panel were professionals. My mom was a social worker by training. One woman was a pediatrician on the University of Minnesota faculty; the other was the first female visual communications specialist for 3M Business Products. Another was not employed outside the house. At one point in the interview the housewife stated, "personally, I'd rather work for a man,"[7] and claimed she had achieved a harmony between domesticity and political involvement in the community. The interviewer, Sylvia Chessen, probed the women on gender roles. My mom compared it to racism, making an analogy that pointed out an irony history perpetuates. Women in literature are invariably depicted in a discriminatory fashion while racism strives to avoid old stereotypes. She spoke of the recent withdrawal of books from libraries that depict Native Americans in a discriminatory fashion. "If they started withdrawing all the books that discriminated against women, we wouldn't have any books in the library." She said it (the views of women) "will depend on how mothers and fathers today bring up their children, on the values that are encouraged."[8]

In 1973, at Central Elementary, my mom took it upon herself to reverse a situation that taught stereotypical gender roles. A group of boys were behaving badly, and the school psychologist began to counsel them. In an attempt nurture their egos, the male students were placed in an exclusive class. Parents were deceived, and they were led to believe that, reciprocally, there must also be a girls class and a mixed class. My mom pointed out the stereotypical activities in which each unisex group was taught to engage. Parents objected and put enough pressure on the school's principal that a meeting was called. Suspiciously, the meeting was scheduled for the middle of the school day when many parents worked and could not attend. My mom was working part-time at the University of Minnesota's Department of Educational Psychology and was able to attend the meeting. She was surprised to find that many complaints were from parents of the kids in the co-ed classes. They felt their children were being denied something, possibly essential life lessons that the segregated kids were learning.

A teachable moment availed itself, and my mom seized it. However, she was the only parent to address the issue of stereotyping. After the meeting the principal requested to talk privately with my mom sometime. Sometime never came. My mom called the school and arranged a meeting with the principal. Most of the meeting consisted of the principal telling of her own frustrations. Having a long career as a nurse in the women's air corp during WWII, she now aspired to be a doctor. Clearly the principal was projecting her own issues to defend the gender situation going on in her school.

Richfield's affluent rival, Edina, had produced a pom-pom waving, baton twirling teacher for District 280 (my mom did reluctantly buy Susan a baton for her class). The teacher's heart was in the right place, she just had no clue of the lasting effects teaching stereotypical gender roles to fifth graders might have. The young teacher was ignorant but gracious and allowed my mom to enlighten her students.

"I got a copy of the *Weekly Reader Edition* for each girl that focused on women in the world of work."[9]

The readers came in teacher's editions. They were small, rectangular booklets. One began with the story of Pocahontas. It questioned whether the young Native American woman would be remembered in history if she had saved the life of a woman rather than that of Captain John Smith, a notable white man.

Newstime

WOMEN's LIB
What do you think of the movement?
How do other students feel?
How did the movement start and
Where is it going? Who are its
leaders? For answers to these
And other questions, read on.

The cover depicted a few women of color. Women protested for equality in employment. One frame had a female traffic officer. Betty Friedan, Kate Millet, Martha Griffith and Gloria Steinem were prominent in the pamphlet. My mom also used an audio aide. From 1972 to 1974 Arvonne Fraser was president of the Women's Equity League. She hosted a fifteen minute program on MPR that focused on women in areas of work usually filled by men. For two weeks, every day, Fraser's progressive ideas were heard by girls at Central Elementary. Finally, it was time to go into the lab. My mom's impromptu course in gender equality ended with meeting some people who had gone outside gender lines. She brought three guest speakers to the classroom; they included Joan Growe (state representative for legislative district 40A), a female pharmacist and a house husband.

Light infiltrated unisex rooms, and my mom's message found a pocket somewhere in the air of disinfectants the male janitors used. Gender segregation was never again proposed in Richfield's public schools. My mom doubts the integration had a lot to do with the booklets and speakers. Her assumption was that it was mostly the parents' objections to the separation and their suspicion that one group was learning something that the other wasn't. The girls' teacher gave her baton a much needed rest and the boys' teacher went back to teaching multiplication. In the end, my mom's equality lessons of the 1973 to 1974 school year were, at best, subliminal messages for the future.

Television was even presented to us in a family way that was designed, either by plan or coincidence, to enlighten us on society's inequalities. We learned from *All in the Family.* Every Saturday night at eight o'clock all in our family gathered together to watch. The cleverly scripted exaggeration of bigotry and chauvinism hit us like a brick wall. These ideas were just stepping out of hiding places in society, and Archie Bunker displayed them to us in palatable, comedic forms. We were encouraged to join our parents to watch the mini-series *Roots. Saturday Night Live* premiered in October 1975. As a family we watched parodies of racial stereotypes and slurs.

Chapter Eleven

Reconciliations

"Shake it up... make it change in order for it to survive. It's not necessary to dump it. Only make it work."
—Shirley Chisholm

More than a century before those words were said a few women did shake things to "make it change" someday. In 1872 Victoria Woodhull became the first woman to run for the presidential nomination. She was nominated at New York's Apollo Hall by the Equal Rights Party. Woodhull was on a ticket with statesman and orator Frederick Douglas as vice presidential nominee.[1]

From 1830 to the years of reconstruction, African-American men and women and white women held significant roles at conventions. Through much of the nineteenth century free and fugitive blacks gathered at infrequent state and national conventions. They plotted courses of how they could achieve educational, labor and legal justice.

In 1855 Philadelphia hosted a Colored Convention. One of the delegates to that convention was a young African-American woman named Mary A. Shadd. However, in the nineteenth century, only three women were acknowledged as official delegates; Shadd, Elizabeth Armstrong and Rachel Cliff at 1855's National Colored Convention. Cliff was employed as a *janitrix* or janitress while active in the Colored Conventions Movement.[2] The first female delegates to major parties' national conventions did not occur until 1900. In Philadelphia's Exposition Auditorium, Frances Warren cast her vote with 926 delegates to unanimously nominate William McKinley for president and Theodore Roosevelt for vice president at the Republican National Convention. That same year, in Kansas City, Missouri, Elizabeth Cohen was a delegate to the Democratic National Convention. After another delegate from Utah could not serve, Cohen seconded the nomination of William Jennings Bryan for president and Adlai E. Stevenson I for vice president.

The push for women's suffrage shifted to the northwestern United States at the end of the nineteenth century. Jeannette Rankin earned women the right to legally vote in the states of Washington and Montana. Speaking before the Montana legislature, Rankin proposed a plan to obtain suffrage. In November 1914, Montana passed an amendment to its constitution that gave women unrestricted voting rights. Throughout 1915 she campaigned for one of the two seats in Montana's one congressional district. Rankin won by over 75,000 votes, and she became the first female member of the United States Congress—four years before the nineteenth amendment was passed.

Ψ

Barbara Amram once gave an interview to the *Richfield Sun.* It was at a time when she held the position of Hennepin County DFL Chairwoman:

"...and with the quiet authoritative voice of one whose convictions have jelled, Barbara Amram said she was among those who sought an alternative 'to the Johnson administration' almost a year before Senator Eugene McCarthy tossed his hat into the fray."[3]

In 1968 when Abigal McCarthy campaigned for her husband in Wisconsin, she was asked whether her husband knew she was talking about issues of the time. She said he had sent her there to talk about them. At that time few women influenced their spouse's vote, let alone took a vital interest in politics.

Shirley Chisholm was a founding member of The National Women's Political Caucus (NWPC). It is the only national organization whose sole purpose is to integrate women into all areas of political and public life. In 1968 Chisholm was elected to the US Congress, representing New York's twelfth district. She had defeated Liberal Party candidate James L. Farmer, Jr. to become the first black woman to be elected to the US Congress. Chisholm took stands against weapons development and US involvement in Vietnam. She stood for fair and equal employment and a woman's reproductive freedom. In January 1972, from a Baptist church in Brooklyn, she promised a "bloodless revolution" at July's Democratic National Convention. Chisholm's candidacy was a double first for the Democratic party.[4] She often discouraged the idea that she was "the woman's candidate," in spite of her strong support of their rights. As one of the founding members of 1971's National Women's Political Caucus, she pointed out, "When I ran for the congress, when I ran for president, I met more discrimination because I am a woman than because I am black. Men are men."[5] Chisholm was so outspoken about the suppressed rights of women that some criticized her for her lack of attention to black issues. An example of this occurred when the head of Operation PUSH (People United to Serve Humanity), the Reverend Jesse Jackson, was asked for help getting her name on the ballot. He refused to endorse Chisholm. A petition was circulated to get her name on the ballot, proving to be a difficult task even in the heavily black district of Chicago. Chisholm discovered that her name would appear on the ballot in the Illinois first district primary. She was pleased and had one hundred buttons and twenty bumper stickers sent to Chicago. Her supporters generated $200 in campaign contributions. The Chisholm campaign invested in one thousand buttons, and with the money made selling those paid for advertising and the printing of literature. Chisholm admitted that her campaign was poorly organized from the start. It was underfunded and, in six month of campaigning, used only $300,000 in funds.[6]

The buttons had slogans such as; "CHISHOLM-PRESIDENT OF ALL THE PEOPLE," "Take the CHISHOLM Trail to 1600 Pennsylvania Ave.," "CHISHOLM—READY OR NOT," or "Catalyst for Change- CHISHOLM for PRESIDENT '72." She went wherever she could get on the ballot and volunteers found speaking engagements for her. New York, New Jersey, California, Massachusetts, Minnesota, Michigan and North Carolina were on the trail. She never set foot in Wisconsin but appeared on the ballot. Write-in votes and those coming from delegate candidates,[7] such as in Illinois, pushed her closer to the convention in Miami that summer. In six months Chisholm had managed to get her name on the ballot in eleven primaries, securing the commitment of twenty-eight delegates to vote for her at the national convention.

Early in 1972, after her DFL precinct caucus, Barbara Amram chose to support Shirley Chisholm in her bid for the party's nomination. At the time, her chief concern was maximizing the number of Chisholm delegates to the third district convention in order to elect a delegate or delegates to the national convention in Miami. When she learned that the plan to call third district delegates prior to the convention had broken down, Amram assumed the task. In doing so, she gained a familiarity among delegates. As a result, she advanced to the state convention in Duluth where the Chisholm delegates elected her to represent them at the Democratic National Convention in July.

Ψ

During the summer of 1972, I was still negotiating the hill at the end of Aldrich Avenue. For the most part, our neighbors took little interest in my mom's political dealings. Her support of Chisholm, and her election as a delegate to the convention that summer, was known only among DFL party members. Like most things in politics, she did what she needed to do with the humble hope that her efforts affected the near or distant future. If people took notice, she was appreciative of their commendations. If no one noticed, though, her convictions did not lose any momentum.

I remember living through July. A level of anticipation kept us cool that summer. I counted down the days until my mom received the three minutes of fame on national TV she had incidentally acquired. My dad borrowed a third television set. Sometime in the early 70s we had gotten a color television with a remote. Each of the three major networks—ABC, CBS and NBC—had their own time delay and their own coverage of the convention. We arranged the three sets on the floor in the living room. I created possible settings. In my favorite one, the three of us sat in the security of the dim as a cool breeze tasseled the warmth of a summer night. We watched the three faces of my mom bounce from the rust-colored shag carpet. Sunday July 9 arrived as considered. We brought her to the airport and she boarded a plane. I knew that, upon arrival in Miami, she would be checking into the Monte Carlo Hotel. She told me so. Arriving the day before the convention, she had no trouble collecting her credentials.

Mom and Shirley before convention

Ψ

It was remembered as "a disastrous start to the general election campaign."[8] The 1972 Democratic National Convention (DNC) was the most disputatious political forum since the "Klanbake" of the 1924 DNC,[9] and its sessions often ran from the early evening until dawn. The Democrats' platform items sparked lengthy debate. The Vietnam War, abortion, welfare and court-ordered busing to end racial discrimination topped their agenda. The planks formed the most liberal platform ever adopted by a major party in the United States. It demanded an immediate withdrawal from Vietnam, amnesty for war resisters, an end to military conscription, guaranteed jobs for all Americans and a guaranteed family income well above the poverty level.

The convention chairman was Lawrence F. O'Brien. Yvonne Brathwaite-Burke took the vice-chairwoman seat.[10] South Dakota senator George McGovern was the front-runner for the nomination of his party. Massachusetts Senator Edward Kennedy was first sought after as a vice-presidential running-mate. The spot was taken by Missouri Senator Thomas Eagleton. He was not well known in the delegation to the convention, and balloting for him became somewhat farcical. The position became contentious, and delegates nominated eight people for the position, including Frances "Sissy" Farenthold, the first serious female candidate for the Democratic nomination of vice president.

Balloting continued sleeplessly into the night. Deprivation took a toll, and delegates glibly cast facetious votes. The dead, foreigners and television characters gained notoriety in the Miami Beach Convention Center. A vote for Martha B. Mitchell-wife of the attorney general-was cast. CBS-TV's Roger Mudd and Communist Chairman Mao Tse-tung were mentioned as possible nominees. And, in an ironic lampooning of the ultra-liberal platform of the convention, archetypal bigot Archie Bunker was tossed into the fray.

Delegate vice presidential nomination vote
(Partial list)
Nominee votes cast

Thomas Eagleton	1,742
Frances Farrenhold	405
Endicott Peabody	108
Jimmy Carter	30
Shirley Chisholm	20
Edward Kennedy	15
César Chávez	5
Wilbur Mills	5

Wendell Anderson	4
Eugene McCarthy	3
Roger Mudd	2
Edmund Muskie	2
Abraham Ribicoff	2
Julian Bond	1
Archibald Bunker	1
George Wallace	1
Benjamin Spock	1
Jerry Rubin	1
Ralph Nadar	1
Martha Mitchell	1
Mao Tse-tung	1
Allard Lowenstein	1
Eleanor McGovern	1
Marth Griffiths	1

Media purposes required that the convention be aired in prime television time. In order for that to happen, with the convention also being seen in prime time on the west coast, the convention could not start until ten p.m. in Florida's eastern time zone. It was 1:40 a.m. in Miami when Eagleton was finally confirmed for the vice presidential spot. For us, in Minnesota, it was 12:40 a.m. On the west coast the clocks read 10:40 p.m. Time zones were tweaked for TV magic. The real delay, as well as the time delay, caused the acceptance speeches of the nominees to be delivered much past "prime" television hours. Pundits speculated that McGovern's campaign was adversely affected by what came to be called the "convention bounce."[11] Following the convention the polling statistics showed that McGovern's support remained unchanged. Following the Republican convention, at the same venue the following month, Richard Nixon garnered a seven point bounce.

Democratic Convention Bounces (in last three presidential elections)

Election	Candidate	Bounce
1972	McGovern/Nixon	0
1968	Humphrey/Nixon	2
1964	Johnson/Goldwater	3

For the Democrats, 1972's convention lacked the protests and violence of 1968. It was the Republican's turn. Vietnam veterans protested the RNC, one being led by activist Ron Kovic. Much of the 'sickness' in the Democratic party that Alpha Smaby had noticed in Chicago had been allowed to heal. A safeguard against racketeering and strong-arm politics had been set in place by The Commission on Party Structure and Delegate Selection. Following Nixon's 1968 electoral victory, a twenty-eight-member commission was designated by Senator Fred Harris, D-Oklahoma, then chairman of the DNC. The commission regulated the nomination process, preventing incumbent candidates (like Hubert Humphrey) from winning their party's nomination without campaigning in primary races. The commission was headed by Senator McGovern, and later by US Representative Don Fraser. It was designed to broaden the participation and bring equal representation for minorities. The McGovern-Fraser Commission implemented eight basic rules and safeguards to the political process:

- The prohibition of proxy voting. This was the practice of members of a decision-making body delegating their voting power to other members of the same party to vote in their absence.
- An end to the unit rule or "winner-take-all" primaries, and other such tactics designed to influence voting.
- A change in the requirements for a quorum (the number

of members required by Robert's Rules of Order to ensure equal representation). No less than 40 percent were required at all party meetings.

- There was no more mandatory assessment of delegates.
- Fees to participate in the process were capped at $10.
- Party meetings that chose non-rural locals were to have uniform dates and times.

Items previously avoided on political agendas such as abortion and gay rights earned their place as subjects of future debate. Organized labor and big-city political machines dwindled in their representation at conventions. George McGovern had organized a grassroots campaign during the presidential primaries to bring delegates to Miami.

- Protests and any political upheaval had to be in easily accessible places and have sufficient notice to the public.
- Quotas mandated that an agreed upon percentage of delegates be female or members of a minority group.

Ψ

The temperature was eighty-six. Humidity seethed outside the Miami Convention Center. A swim in the ocean, or a bite at a diner appealed to conventioneers. They exited the center to be wrapped in the sponge of Florida's dawn. The lights across Biscayne Bay twinkled in the distance. Black head gulls strafed the Atlantic against a rising sun. They scavenged the odd fish. From Dade Boulevard the red staggered letters of a "SAMBOS" sign peered out in the night. Political correctness had deemed the name racist, saying that it was a pejorative term to blacks. The slur was rooted in Helen Bannerman's 1899 book *The Story of Little Black Sambo.* My mom walked farther on Dade, pitting her hunger against her ethics. She went farther from the convention center and found nothing open. However, she *was* in the Deep South, and a restaurant feeding a stereotype was to be expected. She went back to Sambos. The entire Chisholm campaign staff was seated inside!

Ψ

Delegate Vote for Presidential Nomination

Nominee	**Votes**
George McGovern	1,729
Henry M. Jackson	525
George Wallace	382
Shirley Chisholm	152
Terry Sanford	78
Hubert Humphrey	67
Wilbur Mills	34
Edmund Muskie	25
Edward Kennedy	13
Wayne Hays	5
Eugene McCarthy	2
Ramsey Clark	1
Walter Mondale	1

Moments before Amram spoke, she gave her vote to a black alternate voter named Rosalie Davis. Also casting ballots that night were Charles Evers[12] and Percy Sutton, who also made nominating speeches for Chisholm.

Ψ

Now a highly educated seven-year-old, I reasoned to relish the thought of the binocular woman's reaction to knowing her neighbor was nominating a black woman to run the country. I highly doubt she knew or would care. It amused me to consider it though. There lay a cumulative feeling in front of the television sets. All the calling and work my mom had done for congresswoman Chisholm was summed in black and white—and in color. Her dress's lapel proudly offered a WILPH button. To me it stood for the backlog of politics. Reflected in it were the jack-o-lantern plants and dried up money trees. I now heard every solicitous phone call I had once blotted out, from Gene to Shirley. When her bit began, it was surreal. Out of the endless stream of anonymous faces, we saw a face we'd seen all our young lives. She stepped to the convention podium, and in a voice with a register and passion reminiscent of Eleanor Roosevelt, she calmly began to speak:

"It is with a great sense of pride and excitement that I second the nomination of Shirley Chisholm as the Democratic Party candidate for the presidency of the United States. I do so because Shirley Chisholm speaks for the re-humanization of this nation, a renaissance of human values, of brotherhood and sisterhood, human freedom and dignity for all…"

Further into the speech Kennedy's inaugural address was quoted. JFK once called on this nation to "bear the burden of a long twilight struggle, year in and year out, rejoicing in hope, patient in tribulation in a struggle against the common enemies of man; tyranny, poverty, disease and war itself." She concluded that now, a decade later, "…twilight is gone, darkness is falling on families without adequate income security, health care and equal education." She spoke of the unemployed, heads of households that accepted non-existent jobs and the mothers promised non-existent day care centers. More than a decade later the "enemies of man" Kennedy had enumerated were still in need of elimination.

"Tyranny still reigns in a land were bloody nighttime raids are made on blacks, where unarmed students are shot down, where guards and prisoners are slaughtered, where demonstrators in the nation's capital are arrested and herded behind barbed wire and where an innocent black woman is incarcerated for many long months without bail."

Her words came through with a random syllabic precision that mended peacefully among the delays of the three networks. My mom was one of eight Chisholm delegates sent from Minnesota, a state with a black population of less than one percent. Senator McCarthy was referenced only once:

> "Twilight is gone and patience is running out. In the early evening of 1968, a breath of fresh air from Minnesota, Eugene McCarthy, tried to turn the lights on."

Censors had edited out other mentions of him in the speech. Like McCarthy, Chisholm believed in the system. However, she intended only to "shake it up… make it change in order for the world to survive." Where Allard Lowenstein had found it necessary to dump a president who refused to listen, Chisholm found it unnecessary. She proposed that we just make it work. The speech ended with the refrain from Dylan Thomas's poem "Do Not Go Gentle Into That Good Night," leaving an assurance of the continued fight for justice.

Ψ

The system did not work—for us anyway. In the largest landslide since 1964, Richard Nixon defeated George McGovern. Shirley sure did shake it though. She shook it perhaps with the future of women who scratch at that metaphorically encumbered glass ceiling in mind. (I did think of my mom, and the microcosmic role she'd assumed, when Hillary took the stage at the 2016 DNC.)

1972 Presidential Election

Presidential candidate/Party	Electoral votes	Popular vote	%
Richard M Nixon, Republican	520	47,168,710	60.67%
George S. McGovern, Democrat	17	29,173,222	37.52%
John G. Schmitz, American Independent	0	1,100,868	1.42%
John Hospers-Libertarian	1	3,674	0.00%
Linda Jenness-Socialist	0	83,380	0.11%

The shelf-life of chauvinism fights expiration. Remarks are made with bits of pith. They're clean off righteous cuffs with the notion they'll be soft-peddled or go by unnoticed. After the convention, when a woman had stood where many men had stood before, a journalist made a remark for which he should have bit his tongue. He began his interview with Barbara Amram with the question, "what does your husband do for a living?" Advantage Amram; she responded with a question the young journalist had not anticipated. Always the feminist, regardless of what impudence may do to her own reputation, she seized the opportunity to teach a lesson aimed at a male-dominated profession. She asked, "If you were interviewing a man would you ask what his wife did?" It might have been a valid question, with the reporter not presuming anything. However, *Mrs*. Fred Amram was a delegate to the Democratic National Convention, and what Mr. Barbara Amram did for a living was not relevant. The question was non-sequiturial, condescending and desperately sought a context in which to fit.

Fame was fleeting. Isolated areas of the US and Canada sent fan mail. Long-lost relatives called, some friends and one war resister dropped congratulatory notes in the mail. In the context of Shirley Chisholm and the 1972 convention, political historians may remember the name Barbara Amram. She is mentioned in a few obscure online articles, always with the common misspelling of our name,"Amran."

Chapter Twelve

A Silence That's Always Heard

If anything, the citation was destined to be a footnote in city records. My parents were recognized for their activism in Richfield. The moral compasses, passions and sensibilities born out of their respective upbringings were honored January 28, 1974. The mayor of Richfield, Loren Law, came to our house carrying a framed letter recognizing the Amrams for their contribution to human rights in Richfield. It was signed by Law, Maury Haddox—chairperson of the human rights commission—and all of the city council members. The letter was also signed by the other members of the human rights commission.

Photo courtesy of the *Richfield Sun*

Ψ

The errant milk-soaked Apple Jack fell from my spoon. I feigned an interest in the Watergate scandal and left for school that day apprised of current events. Key figures in Wounded Knee, Watergate or the Symbionese Liberation Army meant more to me than they did to most nine-year-olds. Dennis Banks, Russell Means, Patty Hearst, F. Lee Bailey, John Mitchell and Deep Throat roamed my head in resonant monologues. I eavesdropped on the radio, curious to hear what grand plan exceeded the insult of breaking into Democratic headquarters. I listened to understand the motives of our rivals and instinctively rooted for the foils of the Grand Old Party.

Harry Robbins "Bob" Haldeman's (Nixon's White House chief-of-staff) supporting role in Watergate landed him an eighteen-month prison sentence. He was convicted of perjury, conspiracy and obstruction of justice. John D. Ehrlichman was Nixon's counsel and assistant regarding domestic affairs. He was convicted of the same charges as Haldeman. Ehrlichman spent only sixteen months in the pokey. John N. Mitchell, Nixon's attorney general, was convicted of perjury, conspiracy and obstruction of justice, serving nineteen months. John W. Dean was White House counsel to Nixon. The FBI referred to him as "the master manipulator of the cover-up." Dean pled guilty to obstruction of justice, serving the least time.

In 1973 the four key figures in the Watergate scandal were memorialized in song. I listened to it on Minnesota Public Radio during breakfast. It was on the Boone and Erickson show on WCCO and broadcaster Steve Cannon's "The Cannon Mess," in the evening at the cabin. I remember hearing it on sultry afternoons. Dragonflies bounced off the bay window's rusty screens and made a *pinging* sound. It meshed with the far away slams of screen doors on cabins across Tame Fish Lake, echoing when waterskiers went in for lunch. The satirical song "Haldeman, Ehrlichman, Mitchell and Dean" stayed in my head as a mnemonic device. It was performed by

"The CREEP," an acronym for committee to rip-off each and every politician.[1] It sent up the key players of the scandal that had begun in the summer of 1972.

> "We're Haldeman, Ehrlichman, Mitchell and Dean
> The way we've been treated is really obscene
> To think that a bug worth hardly a shrug
> Could end up by getting us tossed in the jug..."

A year after the song was released, Nixon resigned from office. On August 9, 1974, he walked a red carpet to Marine One on the south lawn of the White House. He raised his arms over his head in the peace sign, smiling widely as he ducked inside the helicopter and ascended from the White House lawn to meet his destiny—political exile.

The floor at the cabin smelled smoky. Ash smeared the hearth where I lay on the thin green carpet. Dry and uninspiring, words of our 37th president drifted out over the lake into the setting sun. There were attempts to win a better page in history books by quoting Teddy Roosevelt. The quote was about a man all full of mud and blood. By the end of the speech, loons called lonesomely, while Nixon droned on futilely about the man in the arena who strives, in spite of his short-comings, because there is no effort without error. I pictured him gathering up his index cards from his oval office desk and sulking away like the loons' calls faded into the horizon.

Ψ

Within the walls and levels of our house on Lyndale Avenue, sounds always found better amplifiers. Twenty-six-inch speakers bookended a Krakauer piano. In the corner of the room a Realistic stereo receiver and turntable sat in an antique cabinet. It was at the end of the house in a room where people read, and my mom showcased her best antiques. The stereo was also wired to smaller speakers downstairs. They were on ledges, above the bar.

Sunday mornings came with a ritual. My dad sat in a pea-green-cushioned wooden rocking chair. He read the paper thoroughly with an established order. He got upset if the order was altered. Mostly I did nothing to upset the rhythms of Sunday morning.

The piano got daily use. Susan took lessons, gave recitals and really became quite accomplished. Sheet music from the *Sound of Music*, Fleetwood Mac's *Rumors* and Scott Joplin's *The Entertainer* filled the orange-covered piano bench. She read music with an unparalleled precision and had a working knowledge of the few things every good boy always did fine. Beethoven's *Für Elise* was played infinitely. As I went to bed on school nights, I heard her play. I listened to the notes echo through the house and lay awake until the piano stopped. The hallway light flicked on under my door, and then I heard her door tap shut across the hall. I turned and went to sleep.

Still finding my balance, I was often on the floor with our second dog. I felt it vibrate with the erratic jazz of Dave Brubeck. I listened to Marlo Thomas and friends metaphorically weave their way through the "acts" of *Free to Be... You and Me,* or looked up skeptically when Gil Scott-Heron told us the revolution would not be televised. On rare occasions, usually when local politics was not going well, my parents brought up their coveted Pete Seeger records from a basement cabinet. I heard Pete or Woody Guthrie sing about the union worker, the hobo or the Philadelphia lawyer. Seeger's words of hope, rallying cry and tempo-charged banjo picking buoyed spirits.

Ψ

In July of 1969, 814 soldiers had been the first of 25,000 troops withdrawn to end the US involvement in Vietnam. In January 1973 President Nixon had called for the halt of offensive actions against North Vietnam. The war's curators were cautiously pessimistic, replicating the bogus intent to end the war in order to politicize it. When Gerald Ford assumed the presidency, the hope of ending the war with honor had all but been abandoned. Resources were shrinking. Funding for the ARVN was rapidly diminishing. Politically and economically the war had run its course.

In October 1973, after Egypt's Yom Kippur War on Israel, oil prices had skyrocketed and stunted South Vietnam's economy. Land won was lost and reserved again for the victor. The game of ground acquisition in parallels of longitude began again. Viet Cong forces resumed offensive attacks, again taking advantage of the dry season. In the year of the cease-fire, the South Vietnamese had suffered 25,000 casualties.

When Nixon left office in August 1974, Congress had significantly cut financial aid to South Vietnam. In December that year the province of Phuóc Long was attacked by the North Vietnamese, and its capital city fell in weeks. President Ford tried to persuade Congress to assist South Vietnam before it was overtaken. South

Vietnam had the military might, but they lacked the finances, while North Vietnam was getting financial support from Communist bloc countries. Backing for the war was not finding approval so easily. Congress had gained more Democrats in the mid-term elections.

The Vietnam War is classified as a Cold-War-era proxy war. It began as a conflict between two nations—North and South Vietnam—in which neither combatant directly engaged the other. Such wars rarely yield conclusive victories. The dependent nature of this type of war is conducive to betrayal. On April 21, 1975, South Vietnamese president Nguyên Văn Thiêu resigned as US Forces withdrew toward Saigon. The tearful leader claimed the U.S. Secretary of State Henry Kissinger had tricked him into signing the Paris Peace Accord two years earlier. There were empty promises of financial and military aid. Earlier in April, Ford had asked congress for a $722 million supplemental military aid package, plus $250 million in economic and refugee aid. Congress did not approve.

By April 27, 1975, one hundred thousand troops surrounded Saigon. The ARVN had few defenders left and the city's fate was sealed. Saigon's airport was disabled by the North Vietnamese army and massive numbers of civilians had no way out. Operation Frequent Wind was the name given to what was the last of four plans, or options, for emergency evacuation of Saigon. Carried out by the US Marines' Ninth Division, on April 29–30, it evacuated more than seven thousand at-risk American civilians and Vietnamese from Saigon. President Ford went on television April 23 to say that the Vietnam War, and US aid, was over. Mere hours after the last US helicopter left the embassy in Saigon, the NVA raised the Viet Cong flag above the Independence Palace, and Duong Van Minh, president of the Republic of Vietnam, surrendered to communist forces. Almost two million South Vietnamese military and civilian personnel were dead or wounded, and 361,864 American soldiers were dead or wounded. That number does not include the losses of our allies—South Korea, Australia, New Zealand, Thailand and the Philippines.

Yes, the US won the war for South Vietnam—long enough to get itself and thousands of nationals out. There was no honor, and Saigon became the scene of a mass exodus. Hoards of refugees hanging from helicopters is not how America teaches kids wars are won. The US found a way out of the jungles they had burned for nineteen years, five months, four weeks and one day. I had aged ten years. I had ended one and begun another childhood as those close to me worked vigilantly to end the war. I was adopted by a couple who supported a man who campaigned to be president promising to do so. McCarthy was pragmatic. But he vowed to end it unmitigatedly—regardless of what dominoes fell or what might become of America's reputation. To most ten-year-olds, though, games—particularly games in which America is a player—were not projected to end that way. What I took away from being raised in an environment so close to the democratic process were lessons that said it is possible to be a patriotic American without feeling required to pledge every morning or fly a flag from your house. We live in and maintain a democracy *because* people can be inclined to stand up for what's right and for what's not right, including a presidency or a war. Participating in democracy—voting and going to your precinct caucus—were displayed to me as worthy methods of being a good American. I watched McCarthy supporters drop literature. When I was able, I dropped literature myself. The circumstances that arose from the environment opposing the Vietnam War taught me humility. I was instilled with the belief that America did not always need to be the winners or even the side to take offensive action. A friend of mine, whose parents were not at all active in politics, says he best remembers images of helicopters leaving from the roof of the US Embassy. He recalled how a marine shot at a Vietnamese National hanging on an overcrowded helicopter. My memories are of the fight to end the war here in America. I remember the hopeless feeling as the war went on and on as resolution after resolution to end it was ignored.

Ψ

"If any of you are secret poets, the best way to break
into print is to run for the presidency"
- Gene McCarthy, 1968

A passage from Ecclesiastes in the Hebrew testament claims there is a time to reap and a time to sow. It was a mid-term election year, and in the spring of 1974 the DFL party sowed the remnants of its efforts to elect Senator George McGovern president two years earlier. From her position on the third district executive committee, Barbara Amram suggested an event requiring low overhead as a fundraiser. The idea of Gene McCarthy reading his poetry was discussed. People loved the idea of the party's own anti-war candidate reading his work. Anti-war, as a movement, was not at all the idea of the event. Amram suggested they have it at someone's home and have food donated. She never offered her home, but in the end it was chosen for the event.

Ψ

Mimeograph machines turned, producing paper fliers that were tacked to U of M campus phone poles. Student union bulletin boards at the U of M advertised a poetry reading by Eugene McCarthy. The announcement was seen all around Minneapolis and Richfield:

THIRD DISTRICT DFL PARTY
An Evening of
"Poetry and Politics"
with
Senator Eugene McCarthy
Friday, April 19, 8 PM donation $5.00
Amrams, 7026 Lyndale So
Special Guests: DFL elected officials and candidates

Near sixty-degree weather lasted through the week. Dirty snow melted under the eaves of our house. It formed clumps that cooled in shadows. Funders arrived in Richfield eager to see and hear Gene or just support the DFL. Cars were double parked along Augsburg Avenue. Blocking off our driveway gave us an exit strategy. Elected officials, DFL Party members, poetry enthusiasts, some of my dad's university students and faculty swaggered down 71st street. Arrangements had been made with Oak Grove Lutheran church for overflow parking. The church and its lot were across Lyndale Avenue from our house. From our open door I watched people come in masses. They came by twos or by ones or in groups. They rarely rang the bell and entered through many of the doors including the garage and side doors. Some just stayed on the lawn. I think this was the time someone tried to enter by the fake door on the right.

Additional speakers were wired to the stereo and propped along the wrought-iron railing that surrounded the stairwell, and two were put on the front lawn. The basement, with the various antiques on display, was the first area to fill to capacity. The better-known politicians gravitated toward the basement. They wore leisure suits and sideburns that slimmed their faces. They were trimmed just enough so people still wanted to shake their hand. Long-haired women in jeans and funny political T-shirts wandered upstairs and politely went outside to smoke, although most smoked whichever way the wind didn't blow. People filled the lawn and the two-car garage. The garage had been emptied and was used as a space for making sandwiches. People, with no genuine interest in hearing the poetry, mingled in the garage. Gene could be heard anywhere, but hearing poetry is not *listening* to poetry. My guess is that some people attended just because it was Gene McCarthy, and maybe even because it was McCarthy and other political officials at the Amrams' house.

People came in droves, and I listened for the rattling tin sound of the front door with its intermittent breaks. We counted three hundred people that night.

"People enjoyed hearing McCarthy even if under uncomfortable circumstances," my mom remembers.

The list of party members was long. Notables included:

- Rudy Perpich (Lieutenant Governor from 1971 to 1976; Governor from 1976 to 1991)
- George Latimer (a lawyer who served as St. Paul's mayor from 1976 to 1990)
- Don Fraser (Member of US House of Representatives from Minnesota's fifth district, 1963 to 1979)
- Arvonne Fraser (national president of the Women's Equity Action League, 1972 to 1974)
- Warren Spannus (Minnesota Attorney General, 1971-1983)
- Joan Grow (member of Minnesota House of Representatives representing District 40A, 1973-1974; Minnesota Secretary of State, 1975-1999)
- Emily Ann Staples (ran unsuccessfully as the DFL–endorsed candidate for the Minnesota House of Representatives in 1974; state senator for District 43, 1977-1981)

Concern was given to the dram shop law in Minnesota. Five–dollar tickets were sold to purchase drinks. My mom worried about drivers that left intoxicated. She worried if they were stopped they would tell the police where they had purchased alcohol for a worthy cause. My dad's chief concern was the structure of the house. The weight of three hundred people is a lot for a 2,200-square-foot house. He worried about the floor collapsing. People were constantly going up and down the stairs, looking for the best place to hear or see McCarthy. The back room—the upstairs addition was used as a bedroom—doubled as a second bar. People crowded into the room and lined around the corner to the kitchen.

Somewhere in the chaos my mom worked diligently. I squinted through the chattering maws of beer–scented breath. I fathomed the mutton–chopped profiles and leisure–suited lapels. Gazing past the hazy smoke slicks above long-haired hippie women with complacent yellow-tooth smiles, I identified my mom. She was frantic, but assured, and stood at the dishwasher, kibitzing while loading dishes to be washed. The dining room table was littered with fragmented hot and cold dishes. Various wooden and metal spoons stabbed them with appropriate force. People laughed mechanically and pulled their plates in to themselves at the proper guffaw. I surveyed the faces. They were full of food, wide with smiles and their bites seemed to be interrupted by social unrest.

2174

THIRD DISTRICT DFL PARTY
An Evening of
"Poetry and Politics"
with
SENATOR EUGENE McCARTHY

Friday, April 19, 8:30 Donation $5.00
Amrams, 7026 Lyndale South

Special Guests: DFL elected officials
and candidates

I peered out in the crowd through the sea of the bearded; those who had been previously clean for Gene. Traces of jaw lines appeared on politicians I'd seen on the literature, and I placed them. I had solicited their literature and their ideas. Now they were in person. They were there up close—with an anxious tangibility. Don Fraser or Joan Growe came into view, and I bowed to their minor celebrity. A guest list from that night includes various DFL members, students who worked on Gene's 1968 campaign and the mother of an early *Saturday Night Live* cast member who later went into politics.

The house was a lodge of body heat, but the night was cool. Smoke and an overwhelming staleness caused the windows and doors to be opened. There was a constant flow of traffic, and people wandered, with drink or cigarette in hand, in and out of the house. They meandered up and down the stairs like radio needles searching for the best reception. I don't recall seeing Senator McCarthy much at all. I heard him though. Gene was standing at the wrought-iron railings at the stairway when he began. I think the senator sensed his objective was to get downstairs. He worked the crowd like an adjunct politician with a microphone, gradually making his way through the crowd toward the stairs.

Eventually I tired of the smoke and sardine-like surroundings. In the garage, I whiffed at some fresh air and watched the man who volunteered to make sandwiches. I was nine and fascinated by the production of egg salad and salami sandwiches. The careful rationing of each amazed me. He knew exactly how much egg salad he needed to meet his quota. I kept my ear to the door in our garage that opened to the house, hearing the poetry. The garage door was also open to the night, and a cross breeze of fresh air and cigarette smoke lofted over the sandwiches. I barely heard the house speakers, but still random bits of poetry drifted through the garage into the night. They were lost in the distant swish of Lyndale Avenue's traffic to become the silence that's always heard.

A few loyal souls of the DFL Party stayed after the reading to start the cleanup. A crew of people came to the house the next day. They combed the blue shag carpet in our living room. Cigarette butts and bottle caps filled waste baskets. Garbage bags were filled with paper plates and half-eaten sandwiches. Beer bottles and plastic cups overflowed in bins. The tan, speckled linoleum floor of the rec room was a who's who of the DFL. A better part of the cleanup was spent with razor blade in hand on all fours. Name tags stuck to the floor like patchwork, from the foot of the stairs to the bar. Among the crew was Yvonne Ford from my mom's WILPF days (and my less conscious days). Ashtrays flowed over with the lipstick-stained butts from the more polite cigarette offenders. Susan remembers that the less considerate smokers had snuffed cigarettes out in the red shag carpet of her room. It was a few days before the house smelled right, and the residue of three hundred people evaporated. The event was a success, commercially and critically. Exactly how much money was profited is a lost number. I imagine, though, with the purchase of drink tickets and the five dollar donations we reaped more than was sown. My mom recalls making several trips to the liquor store during the party. The DFL's funds were buoyed, and a candidate for the 1976 election year was ready to be found.

Chapter Thirteen

A Retreat from Politics

Early in the nineteenth century a party of the Sioux tribe returned to Bay Lake. They took their land from an Ojibwa band that was encamped on what came to be known as Battle Point. The lake was called *Ses-sa-beg-a-mah,* which has been translated to mean "Lake of Many Bays," comprising 2,319 acres of northern Minnesota. Long before offensive actions became calculated operations with deafening firepower, canoes were dispatched in silence. The Sioux party came into view a half mile from the tip of the peninsula. The Ojibwa camped on Church Island. The Sioux paddled at dawn, lightly feathering the water into legend. They approached from the southern fringes of the lake. Rays of sun shimmered off the straight black hairs of a young Indian girl as she collected water. She saw the approaching canoes and ran screaming, trying to alert the sleeping elders of the approaching party. She was not fast enough, and the Church Island inhabitants were massacred. The Sioux reclaimed their land.

In 1871 a stop along the Northern Pacific Railroad (NPR) was opened in Withington—the name given to the first stop in Deerwood, Minnesota. The NPR went from Duluth to Washington's Puget Sound. The Wirthington stop piqued anticipation of an industrial center being built on the north shore of Bay Lake. It was free government land, and optimism was high. Withington was the maiden name of the wife of a railway official. The stop was soon renamed Deerwood in the early 1900s for its abundance of deer. The name change also avoided confusion with the Minnesota town of Worthington.

Ψ

In the summer of 1969 my dad was teaching a summer workshop at Macalester College. The program was called Twin Cities Talented Youth. A colleague was selling his cabin, and my dad expressed an interest in buying it. The land was in northern Minnesota, past where Ojibwa elders hit their drums and fried fish on an open grill. The four of us made the first of many treks from the Twin Cities to Bay Lake Township on US 169. Driving straight through in good conditions it took a little over two hours. We passed through the towns of Rogers, Princeton, Zimmerman, Onimia, Millaca and Garrison. I always considered the lake front that is Garrison to be officially *up north.* Bait shops became more frequent. Even if the sign said Dairy Queen, live bait was sold harder than the soft serve. Pedestrians dangled stringers of fish whose gills respired with the lake's tide. The locals appeared to wield an immutable power over the lake's stench. They seemed to know the location of the corpses of dead fish hid in tall grass or marinated on the shore. There was a willingness to live in accordance with what an angler's life offered. A forlorn hesitance lurked in the eyes of the ones that carried lighter stringers that assured them of a better tomorrow. There was an optimism found in being off what were then the grids of today. We were far from Minneapolis or St. Cloud where universities offer much more lucrative, steady employment. I sensed a lifestyle that was more laid-back, still requiring the same work ethic, but independent of anyone's disposable income.

Upon entering the Cyuna Range in Crow Wing County, MN, our maroon station wagon sped into the oblivion of red-tinged ore pits and asphalt hills that sloped and rose like a roller-coaster. We turned onto County Road 10, heeding signs directing us to Bay Lake Township. We stayed at a cabin at Knieff's Shore Acres. Our promised cabin was just down the road from the resort.

Cabin front and back

For $6,600 it wasn't much. Rooted in the earth of one acre of land were many ferns, weeds and poison ivy plants. A dense strip of dandelions lined the grassy median of the driveway. The slanted, sinking—one year it had to be raised—imitation white log cabin at the end of it became my second home. In addition to a main bedroom and a guest room, a three-season porch was used for, what I found to be, the best sleep outside a sensory deprivation chamber. On warm summer nights windows were opened to a line of screening. Cross breezes caressed your face at night, and a symphony of birds woke you with the subtleties of nature in the morning. It was the 'quiet' room where toils of woodpeckers were sometimes heard in the morning, and listening to the calls of loons took place each sunset. The living room had a door on the front and side, although such distinction of them was never made. A fireplace hearth fanned like a seashell, and its cement slab extended out into the room. Sticks and logs were contained in a canvas, tub-like basket. Later, when my parents discovered the weekly auctions in the area, a copper kettle found a use in front of our fireplace. A wooden rocking chair also arrived there, in time, always threatening to rock on our black lab's tail.

The living room blended into the dining area that backed three, screened bayed windows. They looked out on Tame Fish Lake, the smaller, deeper lake, out of which all of our fish came. We had an eight-section dock that ended in a two-sectioned "L." My sister and I often fished from the dock, catching crappies, sunfish and the odd small-mouth bass. My mom, though, took the small rowboat out and brought back northern and walleyes. She always looked serious, like she really knew about fishing. She went solo. Just her, a net and a rod with a fancy spinning reel. A set of four adirondack chairs rested in the yard facing the lake like peeling, sun-burned garden gnomes. Painting the chairs once or twice a summer certainly seemed to be my mom's respite from tackling the various injustices in life. Later, when auctioning began to resemble a form of summer politics, she arduously refinished antique furniture. My dad wrestled with boats and very methodically put in the docks each year. He and my mom split wood with a sledge hammer and a wedge. He read the often picayune news in the local *Crosby Courier*, and, for many summers, walked with me.

I felt far removed from the conceptual time continuum attached to the Twin Cities. Summer days and nights lasted long up north, and a seance to commune with nature was not needed. Each year my dad was given four weeks vacation from the HELP Center. He negotiated to take every Friday and Monday off during the summer. This way he was able to leave work Thursday night and, providing the drive was made in two and a quarter hours, he assured himself Friday at the cabin and often dinner Thursday night. Tuesday mornings I watched him get ready to leave for the week. I ate my breakfast at the table and watched the sun rise over Tame Fish Lake. It was light amber and streamed through the bay window's rusty screen, offering a fresh feel of optimism. My dad assured my mom and me he'd be back Thursday night and carried his brown Samsonite briefcase to the car. While its engine warmed on the cold ground, he wiped the dew from the windshield. I watched the car disappear into the dandelions, and the week was ours to occupy.

My dad's departures and arrivals became routine. They set a metronome to which my summers babbled on optimistically. My mom's early experience as a camp counselor showed. She took us on hikes, canoeing or just into Deerwood to the laundromat mat. The laundry was put in the machines, and we went to get groceries.

"You can pick out two kinds of cereal," she allowed, giving us a vote in our weekly supply.

I grabbed two big boxes of Apple Jacks. Sometimes we emerged from the aisle with a box of Quisp. My mom paid by check for six bags. We each took a bag to the car. The shopping was coordinated with the laundry. Our sojourns into Deerwood were efficient. In the laundromat bored cabin wives milled about with curlers in their hair and chewed gum. They stood at tables in flip-flops and capri pants, folding their laundry in contoured stacks they often put in square baskets of laundry carts. Sometimes my mom tore off the auction fliers on crumbling cork bulletin boards. She quickly inserted her quarters, never seeming as purposeful as the other women, and led us across the street. The Deerwood National Bank—trusted since 1910—was always a stop as the drying cycled. It offered desks with pens chained to them with beaded lanyards. My mom did her banking, and I pocketed several free bank books. They were thin, less than half an inch, and the pages were lined. The cover had a little picture of the bank on it and **FDIC** (Federal Deposit Insurance Corporation) in large bold letters. We used them as notebooks and ledgers.

On the weekends we all went into Brainerd, Aitkin or Crosby. I became acquainted with the small medical center in Crosby. A tic in my ear or a dislocated hip prompted emergency visits to the growing town. In the dog days of summer we went to "Crazy Days" in Crosby or Nisswa. It was the discount days of small town USA. The town was explicitly commercial for the forty-eight-hour duration, prompting banners to be hung. The corners were in coordination with breezes that brushed against signs in shop windows. Antique stores stood complacently on the edge of town to signal the antennae of auction goers to step inside and liberate their treasures. I blinked at the lines. They were the chrome bumpers of flatbed pick-ups shimmering in the sun, nudging one another along the main drag to be the first out of town. We finally paralleled our station wagon in the last parking spot and went into the Ben Franklin five and dime. My dad found the hardware he needed to orchestrate the year's dock removal, and we always found some disposable toy. Brainerd was reserved for the county fair, or just to visit Paul Bunyan's wire tapped recordings that always remembered our names. In Aitkin, my mom knew the bargains on clothes, like corduroy pants, at Butlers.

We were encouraged to read and learn about the world and the country, or simply read without a purpose. Once a week, a bookmobile came lumbering down County 10. The mobile was red, and its tire treads were soft and bare. It parked between our cabin and the neighbor's larger cabin. Inside the mobile was one narrow aisle. We read on rainy days when the fish were more inclined to bite for the lone angler on the lake. The sound of the rain hitting the cabin kept its rhythm. Words in the book began to come faster as if they were pelting our eyes with the same tenacity as the rain. The crackle of the rain drummed softly in my ears, punctuating words with a grammatical flare that only northern Minnesota nature knew. My mom cooked her fish or read the paper in the rocking chair by the fireplace. When she made dinner, KKIN-a station in Aitkin-was on the radio. More often, though, it was a *Prairie Home Companion.* The bluegrass of the Powder Milk Biscuit Band had a taste. I never acquired it. Garrison Keillor's monotone enhanced the hypnotic effects of the rain. Keillor set the bar for us by saying the children of the fictional Lake Wobegon were "all above average." We fell into the below average control group, and our aspiration was told to us on the radio. I took it personally. There was some solace in the notion, though, that we might be better-than-average adults.

My mom was big on projects. Once she asked Susan and me to create a mural. It was on a roll of paper about four feet long. Blues, reds, hues of green and splashes of yellow water color depicted my sister and me canoeing past our dock. Occasionally my mom created something herself. Like political maneuvers, they were always done with humility. She got involved to instruct and encourage us. Although, once she surprised herself. At a hotel weekend—that I walked to—she conceived a future masterpiece. Many small blocks of wood were found in the hotel's parking lot. The idea seemed totally spontaneous on that rainy day at the cabin later, but the work of art was premeditated. She configured the blocks on a textile length of cardboard. It looked like a Rorschach test. The blocks were stacked three high and were spray painted black.

"What is that?" I asked as I began my fifth water color for the Walker Art Center's next exhibit.

"Let's see... oh... I'll call this the Pregnant Roadrunner."

It could have been anything cobbled together for the purpose of instruction. It was good, though, and stood out. It was stark and made a statement. The extemporaneous, spurious name fit. It kind of did resemble a roadrunner, although this one was said to be pregnant and was not futilely pursued by a coyote. The concept was a commentary on the perpetual plot of the Looney Tunes cartoon. Unwittingly, my mom posed the idea of a roadrunner procreating to combat its aggressor (the coyote).

Our cabin was visited by several neighbors, relatives and my dad's HELP Center friends. It hosted Susan's, my mom's and my friends. Some were future political opponents (my mom ran against Ulrich in 1978 for Hennepin County Commissioner).[1] Gertrude Ulrich brought her family of six to our cabin. They stayed in the ten-person tent that accommodated excess guests.

One summer, in the mid-70s, Susan's campfire group came up to the cabin, all nine of them. The group called themselves *Anishinaabe Azikag* which roughly translates in Ojibwa to Wood Tick group. The group was disbanding at the time, and my mom, their leader, asked the nine where they wanted to go for a last trip. They decided on Disney World. Months were filled with bake sales, yard sales and the manufacturing and selling of bizarre crafts. One member's mother grew wild rice, and the group was offered the rejected pieces of the season's yield. Rice was purchased at one dollar and twenty-five cents a pound. Five hundred one pound bags were sold for two dollars each. With the $375 from the rice sales, the profits from bake sales and the selling of crafts, the group was Orlando bound. On June 18, 1976 my mom and her assistant boarded a charter plane with the nine girls. They also visited sights far beyond Disney World such as St. Augustine and Bush Gardens in the two week trip. They worked two years for the trip for which they earned a mention in the Richfield Sun.

Susan and the 8 others before the trip.
Photo courtesy of the *Richfield Sun*

In the later summers, when my metal canes had smaller feet, I spent many Saturday afternoons standing in dusty lots. Auctions were a big hit with my parents. I think it came to them as a negotiable diversion from the rooted and slow growing face value of politics. Items of décor had historic value (hopefully), and I thought my dad, particularly, was intrigued with that aspect. Bidding went fast and the take-away was intoxicating. Auctioneers had a polished patter that rolled off their tongue with twangy pitchfork precision. They wore thin, vinyl cowboy hats and stood like sovereign ministers of commerce in the middle of flatbed trucks. Numerous antiques were brought home to Richfield and became fixtures in the basement. They were eclectic compliments to the growing assortment of political buttons that adorned six bulletin boards. Bedpans, irons, washboards, a second copper kettle (one held wood at the cabin) and a butter churn hung from the walls. They were set on the top of vintage school desks or on the bar. There was a nineteenth century clothes wringer and a wooden barrel from a washer. The barrel was set next to the bar and was used to store the less popular liquor. A green spitoon fit nicely on the step of our bar. A wire rug beater and old railroad lanterns were hung on the walls. My mom brought dressers home to strip and refinish. I built things with Legos in the next room as the pungency of turpentine fumes absorbed the yellow hue that fluorescent lights exude after hours of use. She stripped off the old paint, and it collected in smelly curdled globs. A pastoral gaze crept into my mom's eyes as she hovered over her muse in paint splattered pants and smock.

Wicker-back wheelchair flanked by sheep shearer

The items, though, that drew the most curiosity were placed in the basement like a museum gallery. There was a mannequin dressed in black lace, whose black, pointy-toed, high-heeled shoes sat on shoe trees on the edge of the bar. They resembled shoes that could have been found on the feet of a witch protruding from a precariously grounded cabin.[2] There was a wicker-backed wooden wheelchair and a dentist chair. The latter provided entertainment for our friends. It was acquired from the dental school at the U of M. Above the chair hung a saw and other antiquated farm implements. We vigorously pumped with one foot to raise our 'patients' in the chair. When they reached a sufficient height, we began the cleaning, pretending to use the tools at our disposal.

Silky hair of women circled their heads in thin braids. They wore faded blue jeans, fuzzy ponchos and long leather boots. Pausing as they descended into our den of antiquities, they ducked their heads below the stairwell to peer around the corner. They looked both apprehensive and amused to find a museum in a private home on Lyndale Avenue. Questions were asked of the origins of pieces. The large, wicker-backed, commode-seated wheelchair had an interesting origin. At the time of its acquisition I was walking with small-based metal canes. I stood hunched over them at the auction. The chair was bought up to the auction block to the disinterest of many.

"I'll bid a dollar," my dad called, expecting an opposing bid.

You could have heard a mosquito buzz. Farmers had no use for it. The fact that this man's young son was standing there, with long, disheveled black curly hair, teetering on canes may have influenced the silence. Maybe people thought I needed it.

"One dollar? Surely this fine old chair is worth more than that," the auctioneer prodded, lifting his cowboy hat and scratching his head in wonder. Moments lagged, and the cicada bugs' screech hit its highest bid.

"One dollar, going once, going twice. . .sold, to the man in front."

The chair needed some work. At home my mom set to work patching up the wheelchair. I think she liked the challenge and tangibility her finished product always brought—something politics rarely afforded her.

I'm certain the wicker-backed wheelchair would have fetched much more at Sotheby's. There were no signals at auctions in northern Minnesota, and bidders had no signs to wave. The auctioneers had iron range-weathered faces that were hard to read. Their voices had a register that accelerated at a pace no English accent could catch. Bidders had to know their tongue's worth and when to hold it. To my young ears it became like an *up-north* form of music, staccato sounds incapable of being vocalized south of Garrison. Auctions came to be a rapid-fire sales technique designed to test mental dexterity. The auctioneers, often in teams of two, brothers or father and daughter, gnawed strands of hay or had toothpicks dangling from their mouths. Cowboy hats were worn cleverly to hide their eyes.

"Going once, going twice... sold to the man in the denim overalls."

If a rock was thrown you'd hit one. Nearing the final sale of the auction a subtle humor coaxed the bidders. The last items were almost always oddities people hardly ever went to a store to buy.

"The next item up for bid is... a left-handed bacon stretcher."

Farmers, who were in it to win it, and "summerers," like us, grew silent as the free enterprise system exhibited its versatility. The farmers were serious and had come to the auction with the express purpose of getting a farm necessity. The rest were just anglers, those there with ultimate indifference to what was sold. Sometimes the serious antiquers spotted an item in the flier posted in the Deerwood laundromat. It was an armoire, or a four post bed they pictured hanging out of their truck with red bandannas flying from them.

"One dollar bid and a bid… two and a half, and a four dollar bid and a bid and a ten and a bid and a bid…"

It was flute solo to me. Sometimes, on a whim, my dad suggested that I bid a couple dollars on the "junk boxes." These most often contained enough rusty nails and screws to fill six jars. The boxes had toys, or parts of them, and blocks of wood. We learned creativity at the cabin. The boxes were a diversion from the bed pans and copper kettles. They were a crap-shoot. I found golf balls and old dog tags or fishing tackle. I even recall an old camera. One of the greatest junk box finds was a handicapped parking sign.

On one "cabin stretch" my mom took us into Crosby to see *The Sound of Music.* I was easily frightened by Nazis and Ku Klux Klansmen, men who delighted in raising their arms in a right angle or had an abnormal affinity for hoods. There is one scene where Captain Von Trapp is pursued by members of the National Socialists because he will not serve the Third Reich. The conflict of ethics under the threat of tyranny got me. As a kid, all I saw were swastikas and a man being forced at gunpoint to compromise his ethics. However, it was another film that really scared me.

My mom had taken us to see the 1973 movie *Tom Sawyer.* I remember Tom and Huck finding an adventure in a cave. All night, after the movie, it stormed. I saw Injun Joe's dented and laughing face menacing around the cabin. He was only too happy to engage me, like he had Huck, in a knife fight. Joe persisted. He appeared with a blood-thirsty grin each time I closed my eyes. Joe was outside in the rain. He was inside, in my head, with the rain. The injun had my cavalry of defense mechanisms surrounded. I could not blame it on the driving rain that pummeled the small cabin or the willow's weeping leaves whipping our windows like wipers. I tried to recall some of my favorite things, like Julie Andrews had instructed those Von Trapp kids as it stormed. All I could conjure were raindrops on willows and whiskers on bullheads and Injun Joe's eyes peering from ledges. In the end, tiredness reigned victorious. I roamed the cabin looking for a safe haven. It was nearly four a.m. when I laid down in the porch and found sleep. Soon dawn peeked over Tame Fish Lake, and the wide blades of grass glistened with the night's rain.

I don't recall ever taking rehabilitative walks with my mom. It was a father and son activity. He challenged me. He provided motives such as going to dinner or a motel weekend with the family. There was a buffet in another bay of Bay Lake. Going to eat there was the reward a few times. A nice elderly lady owned the buffet. I endeared myself to her during our frequent visits. My canes and my capacity to eat like someone twice my age singled us out. My dad always asked me, "Are you getting enough to eat?" (Years later he told me the owner made him pay the adult price for me.) More often the reward was a weekend at a motel in Brainerd. It was always important that the hotel have an indoor pool. They were classy, four-star franchises like Best Western or Ramada Inn. Sometimes we combined the motel weekend with our annual pilgrimage to the Crow Wing County fair in Brainerd. I earned a break from walking and was pushed in my wheelchair at the fair. We left the fair when the food in my stomach had been sufficiently churned by the scrambler or the tilt-a-whirl.

Back at the hotel we swam in the indoor pool. We had drinks and bonded in the room before dinner. We were tight as a family unit. The accident, the auctions and the politics all had nourished that bonding, strange as it seemed. We went down to eat in the hotel restaurant after a suitable refreshment. I stepped into the dimly lit halls with shiny shoes and a sport jacket. I had even attempted to tame my "halfro." A lounge band played a cover of "You are the sunshine of my life." The lights of ambiance flooded the surrounding sound. Its members—none of whom tried to be Stevie Wonder—nodded to me as I slowly made my way to our table. I followed the pretty young hostess, feeling suave and invincible. My dad told me to order anything I wanted from the regular menu (I don't recall ever ordering from a kid's menu). When it was time for dessert, I decided to try the house pecan pie. It looked cool enough, and I dug in as soon as it arrived. My scream was heard throughout the restaurant. It was so hot that I burned my tongue. My invincibility was left on that plate.

Summers always ended with gradual finesse, like sunsets, drawn out like the cries of loons. Political wheel-houses began their advance toward November. Priorities shifted, much like the cabin. Our neighbors at the cabin had winterized their retreats. We never did. It was definitely not worth the investment. Our little shanty served its purpose. It was slightly tilted and precariously founded and remained a cabin in the true Minnesota sense. Columbus Day weekend was the scheduled date to close the cabin. My dad took the dock off the lake in a well-orchestrated operation. Posts and sections had their uniform spot. A day was always set aside to wax the speedboat before it was stored at a marina. Dishes were washed, and the freezer was defrosted. Mouse traps and poison were laid out for them after our dog was in the car. Doors were locked, and we set out for Highway 169 the last time for six months.

Chapter Fourteen

Living with the Aftermath

To this day, April 30 remains just a day. A dubious acronym was never assigned to precede it (for example, our calendar notes October 25 was the 1983 invasion of Grenada). Nothing significant, or insignificant, is noted to have occurred April 30, 1975. Life went on without the propensity to protest the war machine that had provided the nation with a reason to challenge authority for nearly twenty years. Countries around the South Pacific did not fall to Communism like a line of dominoes tapped. The Vietnam War was barely mentioned in my high school text books. It was mostly The American Revolution, The Civil War and WWII—the latter replete with the stomach-turning 1956 film *Night and Fog*.

No one at Richfield High School wanted to teach about America's errors in judgment. We were taught about the favorable wars from which a sense of liberty or justice prevailed. Through World War II, war was supported (mostly) and America's record of winning them was relatively sound. After Pearl Harbor, a majority of Americans backed America's involvement in the Pacific theater. Appreciation for the military's service in WWII was rarely questioned. The US had been attacked by a foreign enemy and, on

December 8, 1941, President Roosevelt went before Congress and got approval to declare war on Japan. The president's request to go to war was checked and balanced. The Axis powers of Germany and Italy declared war on the US three days later. We knew our enemies and their histories. Soldiers knew who the enemy was. They always knew they were fighting the armies of Hitler, Hirohito and Mussolini.

Some veterans of WWII gladly tell their stories, often remembering them in precise detail. Most of the Vietnam War veterans I approached for this book were far less likely to reminisce about their experience. With a reluctant sigh they confess, with cold dead eyes. They dredged a distant part of their mind like they were retrieving a long repressed crime. For the draftees who were sent against their will, any trace of pride in what they did was left on the tarmac upon their less than heroic return.

As I became a young adult, America was emancipated and then assassinated. It was eviscerated and left to reconstruct again. When I was just learning about women, I watched as society was emasculated. I learned that women could, and did, make giant leaps for womankind. My mom left the University of Minnesota's Campus Assistance Center to practice social work privately from our house. In 1975 the University of Minnesota saw an influx of refugees. Vietnamese, Laotian, Cambodian and Hmong immigrants arrived on the university's banks eager to learn. They spoke little or no English, and ESL (English as a Second Language) teachers were in high demand. Asian languages were not commonly taught, and the supply of such teachers was short. Faculty at the university met the demand by offering grants for teaching ESL. Unlike the black and Hispanic students who had been demanding more ethnic study courses since the late 60s, the Asians that came were passive. Their reticence often resulted in their needs not being met, and they were encouraged to be more active.

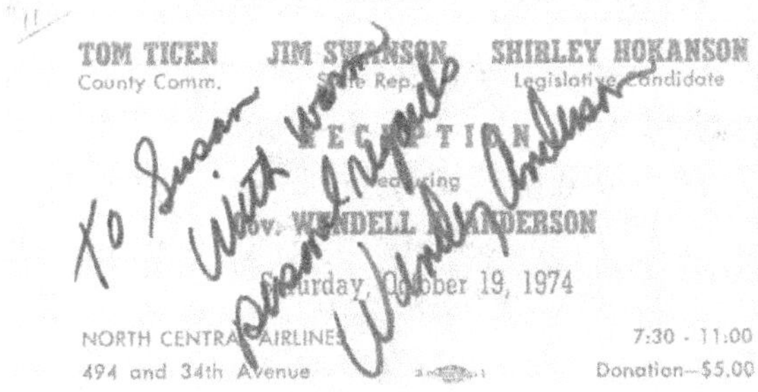

Ticket autographed by the governor

The long political battle was over along with the common relating feel that our family had come to know. The spontaneous optimism that the dollar junk boxes at auctions brought was gone. The animated wisdom of talking bills on *Schoolhouse Rock* (cartoon bills that instruct how they become laws) was gone. Unifying moments like that July night in 1969 were rare. I was a boxing fan, and my dad and I had watched the fights and the fighters weary down. We watched all of Muhammad Ali's fights. I admired his antics and activism out of the ring. Usually, though, he played the pacifist and exhausted his opponents with his patented rope-a-dope. The days of blue-jeaned women in long leather boots and warm, fuzzy ponchos peering curiously around the stairwell at our basement antiques were gone. My sister collected autographs of friends and people she met in the days of fundraisers. They were mementos in a small red book.

My sister's book was a record of how the DFL had shaped our lives. Not long after our house hosted the McCarthy fundraiser, our family attended a reception for mid-term governor Wendell Anderson and a few other candidates and officials.

TOM TICEN JIM SWANSON SHIRLEY HOKANSON
County Comm. State Rep. Legislative Candidate
RECEPTION
Featuring
Gov. WENDELL ANDERSON
Saturday, October 19, 1974
North Central Airlines7:30-11:00
494 and 34th AvenueDonation-$5.00

One parent was always there, fighting the good fight. If it was a long-shot nominating Shirley Chisholm for president, for example, or not buying grapes to one day assist migrant workers, my mom was there. She was there to march at Honeywell or stuff envelopes with literature instructing people on how a war can end. When the "teachable moment" to oil the wheels of gender equality in Richfield schools presented itself, my mom was there. If it was enlightening nuns on caucus proceedings or casting votes for McCarthy as police did their finest Gestapo impressions in Chicago's streets, my dad was there. He was also there for the moments to teach that very often assisted me in my rehabilitation. I see now how everything that was done in the period of 1965 to 1975 directly or indirectly affected what I now see and do. It influenced how I view women, how I vote and how I walk with an eye out for injustices.

In Richfield and in Bay Lake Township, the years I learned to walk again were a time of innocence. The war did not intrude on my dad and me as we walked along Aldrich Avenue or shuffled through the spots of sun peeking from the trees along Tame Fish Lake. The early 1970s were a unique time to grow up in America, particularly in a family where politics was usually next to everything. It was a time for growth; a period in America when dissension for the greater good was a necessary recourse. It was a time of bonding and relaxing. It was a time for education and rehabilitation. It was a time of hotels as rewards and a time for county fairs. It was a time when roadrunners anticipated the worth of their progeny; when invincibility could find humility in a slice of pecan pie. Our country was given the opportunity to examine democracy and, if necessary, to tear it apart and build a better one. But Minnesota witnessed the power of a handful of DFL members. I like to think some lesson was profited from nearly two decades of war. At the very least, the recipe for ending them can be found in an old literature box that's behind the fondue pot under the bar in a dissenting Democrat's basement.

Epilogue

The Dickensian line, "It was the best of times; it was the worst of times," threatened to lie in the margins of my book, scrawled whimsically like a passive footnote. People I interviewed smiled skittishly when asked about the old days in the DFL. Their eyes lit up as they connected names they hadn't considered for decades. They spoke of the back-stabbing and uphill battles, but also of the small victories along the way.

An insidious commonality compelled me to finish writing this book. Memories of a youthful identity tendered my mind; names that floated through the house when I was a kid, names that were tattooed on my brain from bulletin boards of buttons and bumper stickers. Many of the Dissident Democrats from that clandestine dinner party in the fall of 1967 had passed on, leaving their marks in books that might one day be written. Those still living have long since put down any formidable political torch. They rarely questioned the long-term worth of what they did, leaving the fights that come in the twenty-first century for my generation, or the millennials, to tackle. In this memoir, I have attempted to maneuver memories of family and truths of the Vietnam War as fluidly, creatively and with as much instinct as reflective writing allows. Incidents and experiences were not embellished and remain as mundane and pedestrian as I recall them.

Ψ

In September 1974, Gerald Ford began a program of conditional amnesty for scores of draft resisters.[1] Earlier in the month, the president pardoned his predecessor. Ford explained in a speech to the nation that exonerating Nixon of his alleged Watergate crimes was in the best interest of the country. He spoke of the Nixon family situation saying, "It is a tragedy in which we have all played a part. It could go on and on and on or someone must write the end to it. I have concluded that only I can do that and if I can, I must."[2] Critics of Ford condemn his pardoning of Nixon. They speculate that a deal was made *quid pro quo*—a pardon for the presidency. In a mid-term election year Ford became president by default, making him the first person to serve both as vice president and president without being elected to either office.[3]

Today, the Vietnamese refer to that twenty-year "conflict" as the American War or, The Resistance War Against America. On April 30 in Vietnam (the day the last helicopter left the US Embassy in Saigon) the streets are full of public celebration. To be fair, it was our war. In 1954 President Eisenhower had sworn he'd protect South Vietnam from Communist rule. Honoring that commitment was Lyndon Johnson's initial rationale for widening our involvement. Between 1965 and 1975, multiple opportunities for America—or North Vietnam—to end the war were ignored.

A subtle and sanctimonious resonance surrounds the claim "peacekeepers of the world." The peace*keeper* of the world—the ramifications of that phrase seem too consuming to ever be successfully executed. The epic task implied is too daunting to be implemented without compromising someone's integrity. Now where does that leave us for the next altercation, the next belligerent moment in which America can flex its muscle? By reciprocation, that makes every country we've invested in since Vietnam the *war-makers*, or *peace takers.* Lebanon, Nicaragua, Grenada, Iran, Kosovo, Afghanistan, Pakistan, Libya, Israel, Iraq, Syria, Israel, Palestine… the hostilities mount. Majorities of humanity attempt to play war games with unclear objectives. They love to be eternal optimists and continually try the same thing with indifferent results. America's heroics in the field of war, of stepping into potential quagmire situations, of "keeping" peace, or the increasingly popular "nation building" in countries on whom we've forced our way of life, are rarely questioned. But, just as rarely, the minority can convince the majority of its insanity. Bands of rebels, dissidents—those who see things as they ought to be—rise lawfully. They use Roberts Rules of Order and give democracy its day in court. Change most often begins locally. It begins in many, many localities to eventually affect things globally.

Pete Seeger passed away in 2014. He began his political life supporting the progressive ideas of Henry Wallace. When he was called to serve in WWII he went willfully. Eventually he did in the army what he did all his life: he rallied people with his music. Looking at Pete Seeger's life and what I learned writing this book, it is clear to me now what American is. It is also clear what Un-American is. Seeger stated two paths he could have taken when WWII broke out. He could have taken a pacifistic approach, allowing Hitler to annihilate ethnic populations. Rather, he became a Communist and "quarantined the enemy." He didn't become a Marxist Communist, with its focus on class systems and the development of society, but a kind of communist that looked "around" America, past the veils sub-committees love to hang, to really see what was happening. Hitler was a formidable enemy, but to many during the Cold War, Communism was also the enemy. Seeger and scores of others in the activist or entertainment business were branded and ostracized from America. They were not allowed to work. So "American" becomes a relative term. Those with money, fame or a strong sense of justice were banned from anything that might leak un-American ideas to the media. Seeger used to say, "Think globally, but act locally." He said that if any change is going to come, it will not be from one or two large governments or councils. Large changes will come slowly, but it will come because of thousands of smaller ones. That's where I came in—and my very first lesson in anything political was in 1967. I noticed the noise and watched the activities in the third district. The following year I followed my dad to precinct caucuses. He rose through levels to chair committees. Voting booths with the curtains and black levers next to the candidates' names were around before I was old enough to vote. I remember them because I used to watch my mom vote.

At my 2016 precinct caucus, I submitted a resolution to expand the scrutiny and prosecution of those employers who are in violation of the ADA (Americans with Disabilities Act). I attended the next level, the senate district convention. When I watched the Democratic National Convention that summer, the rights and needs of the disabled were addressed. I felt a part of me—of my resolution—was there in Philadelphia. I know my resolution was adopted. It was one of the 152 that made it to the senate district convention. Even if only a seed of that resolution from February remained, I may have changed something. The feeling was incredible. I participated in *making* democracy! Fathoming the macrocosm is enticing.

Ψ

In a final analysis, when Utopias are tossed into the frays and history is sieved through miscalculated operations and assassinations, the conflagrations that bleed better days, presidents will look out over the reflecting pool and beyond Lincoln's memorial. They'll assess the damage that's been done. They'll see the white gravestones that line the horizon, and they might surmise the cost of the wars we fought. And, if they look long enough, they'll see reflected the brave objectors poking flowers into icy stares of guns.

But if I were back home, safe in Richfield, in my old neighborhood, on the steps of our first house where my dad and the neighbor sipped beer, I'd remember the many decades past. I'd remember when wars were hushed and how we worshiped nature to make our summers last. I'd see friends laugh as they are spun from the older girl's tanned arms. In my Utopian world I'd see the flashes of Cronkite codes. I'd hear the crickets' cadence in the night and baseball cards clacking in stingray spokes.

End notes

Chapter One—Several Small Steps

1. Schlesinger, Arthur M, *Robert Kennedy and His Times*, (Ballantine Books, 1978), p. 772
2. Jacobs, Seth, Cold War Mandarin: Ngo Dinh Diem and the origins of America's War in Vietnam, 1950-1963,(Rowman & Littlefield, 2006), p. 2

Chapter Two—Contraindicates

1. Stanley Karnow,*Vietnam: A History*, 2nd ed. (London: Pimlico, 1997), p. 264
2. In 1972, Nixon's margin was wider in his defeat of George McGovern
3. Howard Kaibel II, *Ward Number Six* (New York: Scribner's, 1972), p. 9
4. Ted Smebakken, *Minneapolis Tribune*, August 7, 1966
5. William Tilton in Kenneth E. Tilson's Judging the Judges (Saint Cloud, Minn.: North Star Press (2002) p.15
6. From *The Telegraph*, Senator Eugene McCarthy, (obituary) December 12, 2005
7. Forrest Harris in Alpha Smaby, Political Upheaval: Minnesota and the Vietnam Anti-War Protest (Minneapolis: Dillon Press, 1987), p. 26

8. Ted Smebakken, Minneapolis Star, 1967, in Mary Shepard, ed., *Republican Workshop Bulletin*
9. Lyndon B. Johnson quoted in Daniel Ellsberg, *Secrets: A Memoir of Vietnam and the Pentagon Papers (*New York: The Penguin Group, 2002)
10. Text from Gulf of Tonkin Resolution, August 7,1964
11. Robert Dallek,*Nixon and Kissinger: Partners in Power* (New York:HarperCollins, 2007), pp. 73-74
12. Lyndon Johnson describing the qualities of a personal assistant in *Uncensored Comments of American Politicians*

Chapter Three—A Party Divided

1. Kaibel in Smaby, Political Upheaval, p. 76
2.A global foundation whose mission is the advancement of human welfare
3.McGeorge Bundy in Smaby, Political Upheaval, p. 45
4. Kaibel in Smaby, Political Upheaval, p. 45

Chapter Five—The "Mystic"

1. Reference to an 1821 federal statute in the US regulating slavery in the western territories
2. David McCulloughm, *Truman.* (New York: Simon & Schuster, 1992), p 425
3. *Truman,* 1992, p. 425
4. Hubert H. Humphrey, 1948 Democratic National Convention Address, July 14, 1948, Philadelphia, Pa.
5. A US senator from South Carolina and 1948 presidential candidate for the State's Rights Democratic Party, Thurmond served in the senate from 1956 to 2003, initially as a Democrat and as a Republican after 1964.
6. Steven E. Ambrose, *Eisenhower: Soldier, General of the Army, President-Elect, 1890- 1952* (Delran, N.J.: Simon and Schuster, 1984), p. 175

Chapter Six—The Progressive Gene

1. I met the binoculars woman in recent years and she was still that woman I remembered on Aldrich. I had no trouble believing the stories of her prejudice.

Chapter Seven—Assassinations of Character

1. A liturgical book holding instructions and texts needed to observe the Roman Catholic mass throughout the year.
2. R. Backus, MD, Fairview Hospital medical record, January 19, 1971
3. From an email sent by Yvonne Ford, July 4, 2014

Chapter Eight—When Cats Walk

1. In 1996, at sixty-three, Fred Amram had a heart attack.
2. Jewish noodle dish
3. Letter from journalist Peter Hamil, February 1968
4. President Lyndon Johnson's address to the nation, March 31,1968
5. Ted Van Dyk, *Heroes, Hacks, and Fools: Memoirs from the Political Inside,* (Seattle: University of Washington Press, 2007), p. 74. Lyndon Johnson's son-in-law was fighting in Vietnam.
6. Refers to the August 20-21, 1968 invasion of the Czech Republic by the Soviet Union and Warsaw-Pact countries Bulgaria, Hungary, East Germany, and Poland. Its purpose was to dismantle an attempted coup by Alexander Dubček to reform a Communist regime in Prague.
7. White, The Making of the President 1968, pp. 265-266
8. A candidate is often nominated at the quadrennial national party conventions simply because he or she if from a particular state or region. The idea is to open negotiations between state leaders and leading candidates to win the delegation's support.

9. Channing Phillips was the first African-American to receive votes for the presidential nomination at a Democratic National Convention.
10. Rick Perlstein, *Nixonland: The Rise of a President and the Fracturing of America* (New York: Simon & Schuster, 2008), p. 324.
11. This was a rule under which a delegation to a national political convention casts its entire vote as a unit as determined by a majority vote
12. From "A New Day for America," Hubert Humphrey's acceptance speech at the Democratic National Convention, Aug. 29, 1968.
13. Rowena "Ronnie" Kaibel in Smaby, *Political Upheaval*, p. 299
14. Abraham Ribicoff in David Farber, *Chicago '68* (Chicago: University of Chicago Press, 1988), p. 201
15. On March 7, 1965 an incident known as "bloody Sunday" began as black marchers in pursuit of their right to vote freely were confronted on the Edmund Pettus bridge by Selma, Al. state troopers
16. Judge Julius Hoffman handed Bobby Seal, leader of the Black Panthers, a four-year sentence for sixteen counts of contempt in November, 1969. Seal was subsequently removed for the trial of the Chicago Eight, thus making them seven.
17. Fred Amram in Smaby, *Political Upheaval*, p. 297
18. A report submitted by Daniel Walker, director of the Chicago study team, to the National Commission on the Causes and Prevention of Violence. The report was made public in December, 1968, and summarizes the Chicago Study Team's review of over 20,000 pages of statements from 3,437 eyewitnesses to the convention.

The report is based on 180 hours of film and over 12,000 still photographs.

19. Abigail McCarthy in Smaby, *Political Upheaval*, p. 312
20. Smaby, *Political Upheaval*, p. 313
21. Anna Chennault in Dallek, *Nixon and Kissinger*, pp. 74-75
22. In a U.S. Supreme court decision *(United States v Katz)*it was upheld that a private citizen, in cases of wiretapping, was still protected under the Fourth Amendment. However, warrentless wiretapping, in the interest of national security was permissible. Johnson's administration claimed a special right to conduct such investigation. A FCC law had been in place since 1934 allowing wiretapping, although the law did not legalize the disclosure of information gathered through wiretapping.
23. From "Humphrey's LBJ Boost" in *The Age,* (Melbourne), September 19, 1968: p. 2
24. From "Mr. Humphrey Tippy Toes," *The Victory Advocate,* (Victoria TX), October 3, 1968: p 3.
25. From "Nixon, Humphrey give their views in four-hour telethon from California," *The Bulletin*, Nov. 5, 1968
26. Ellsberg, Secrets: A Memoir of Vietnam and the Pentagon Papers, p. 260

Chapter Nine—The War Machine

1. Megan Gibson, The Toughest Job you'll ever Love: It was originally thought to be a 'haven for draft dodgers,' Time Magazine, September 22, 2011
2. Judge Miles Lord in Tilsen. *Judging the Judges*, p. 33
3. Lord in Tilsen, *Judging the Judges*, p. 34
4. Minneapolis Star editors in Tilsen, Judging the Judges, p. 34

5. John C, Water and Malina Lida,"Muhammad Ali: Exemplar to the World," online at, http://www.americansc.org.uk/Online/Ali.htm, Feb. 20, 2014
6. From a 1967 intelligence report quoted in Ellsberg, *Secrets: A Memoir of Vietnam and the Pentagon Papers*
7. Henry Kissinger, *White House Years,* (Boston: Little, Brown and Co. , 1979), pp. 231-32

Chapter Ten—Motives & Stratagies

1. Taped conversation with Fred Amram, December, 2013
2. Telephone conversation with Barbara Amram, 2014
3. Paraphrased text, "I Have a Dream," August,1963
4. The matzo is hidden by an elder at some point during the Seder. The younger guests are asked to find it in order to complete the Passover meal
5. Text from *Passover Haggadah.*, Hartford, Conn.: Prayer Book Press, 1959)
6. Barbara Amram in Sylvia Chessen, "Liberation: Do Women Want it, Need it?" in *Bloomington Sun-Richfield Sun-Minnesota Valley Sun*, April 23, 1970
7. Ibid.
8. Ibid.
9. Telephone conversation with Barbara Amram, 2014

Chapter Eleven—Reconciliations

1. Douglas was nominated without his knowledge, neither campaigning for nor acknowledging the nomination.
2. The movement consisted of a series of national, regional, and state conventions. In the decades preceding and succeeding the Civil War, the sporadic conventions' delegations were made up of free and fugitive African-American community and religious leaders, businessmen, writers, publishers, and abolitionists.

3. Alys Brockway,"County DFL Chairwoman finds Politics is her Cup of Tea," *Richfield Sun*, 1968
4. Republican Margaret Chase Smith was the first woman to run for the presidential nomination of a major party. She served as Maine's first female U.S Representative (1940 to 1949) and U.S. Senator (1949 to 1973).
5. James Barron, "Shirley Chisholm, 'Unbossed' pioneer in Congress, is Dead at 80," *New York Times,* Jan. 3, 2005
6. Jo Freeman, "Shirley Chisholm's 1972 Presidential Campaign," University of Illinois at Chicago's Womens History project, February 2005
7. Jo Freeman ran for delegate to the 1972 Democratic National Convention with the purpose of putting Shirley Chisholm's name on the ballot. She came in ninth out of the twenty-four candidates, and attended the convention as an alternate with the Chicago Challenge Delegation.
8. David Rosenbaum, "George McGovern Dies at 90, a Liberal Trounced but Never Silenced," *New York Times*, Oct. 21, 2012
9. Klanbake refers to the heated debate over attempts to resurrect the Ku Klux Klan. Taking a record 103 ballots to nominate John W. Davis, the 1924 Democratic National Convention is the longest in U.S. history, running from June 24 to July 9. Davis was defeated by Republican Calvin Coolidge.
10. Yvonne Brathwaite-Burke served as a member of California's State Assembly from the state's 63rd district from 1967 to 1973. She was twice a member of the U.S, House of Representatives, representing California's 37th district from 1973 to 1975 and the state's 28th district from 1975 to 1979
11. Convention "bounce or bump" refers to a slight up-swing of support following a televised convention. The

phenomenon varies greatly, but presidential candidates usually see an initial surge in their polling numbers after the convention.

12. Charles Evers is the brother of African-American civil rights activist Medgar Evers assassinated June 12,1963.

Chapter Twelve—A Silence that's Never Heard

1. The official organization of the Nixon campaign was Committee for the Re-election of the President, or CREEP

Chapter Thirteen—A Retreat from Politics

1. Gertrude Ulrich vied with Barbara Amram for the Democratic nomination for county commissioner in Hennepin County's fifth district. Gertrude won the nomination; she was defeated in the election by Republican Randy Johnson.

Epilogue

1. On January 21, 1977 President Jimmy Carter officially pardoned all Americans who had failed to register for the draft or left the country to avoid service in Vietnam
2. Gerald Ford, "Gerald R. Ford Pardoning Richard Nixon," *Great Speeches Collection,* September, 8,1974
3. Nixon's vice president, Spiro Agnew, resigned Oct. 10, 1973. The scandals leading to his resignation included tax evasion and money laundering. On Nov. 27, the U.S. Senate voted ninety-two to three to confirm U.S. Rep. Gerald Ford of Michigan as vice president

Bibliography

Ambrose, Stephen E. Eisenhower: Soldier, General of the Army, President-Elect, 1890-1952, New York: Simon & Schuster, 1984

Armstrong, Scott, and Bob Woodward. *The Brethren: Inside the Supreme Court,* New York: Avon Books, 1981

Barron, James. "Shirley Chisholm, 'Unbossed' Pioneer in Congress, is Dead at 80," *New York Times,* Jan. 3, 2005

Brockway, Alys. "County DFL Chairwoman Finds Politics is her Cup of Tea," *Richfield Sun*, 1968

Campbell, Joseph. Getting it Wrong: Ten of the Greatest Misreported Stories in American Journalism, Oakland, Calif.: University of California Press, 2010

Chessen, Sylvia. "Liberation: Do Women Want it, Need it?" *Richfield Sun*, April 23, 1970

Dallek, Robert. *Nixon and Kissinger: Partners in Power*, New York: HarperCollins, 2007

Ellsberg, Daniel. Secrets: A Memoir of Vietnam and the Pentagon Papers, London: The Penguin Group, 2002

Faber, David. *Chicago '68*, Chicago,: University of Chicago Press, 1988

Foner, Philip S. History of the Labor Movement in the United States: Postwar Struggles 1918-1920, New York: International Publishers Co, Inc., 1988

Freeman, Jo. "The Chicago Convention: A Baptism Called a Burial," *Moderator*, October, 1968

Freeman, Jo. *A Room at a Time: How Women Entered Party Politics,* Lanham, Md.: Rowman & Littlefield Publishers, 1999

Freeman, Jo. "Shirley Chisholm's 1972 Presidential Campaign," February 2005

Dallek, Robert. *Nixon and Kissinger: Partners in Power*, New York: HarperCollins, 2007

Diaz, Susana, and Claire Peterson. "Exploring the United Farm Workers' History." The Grape Boycott Project, 1996. http://l3d.cs.colorado.edu/systems/agentsheets/New-Vista/grape-boycott/, Feb. 15, 2004

Jacobs, Seth. Cold War Mandarin: Ngo Dinh Diem and the origins of America's War in Vietnam, 1950-1963. Lanham, Maryland: Rowman & Littlefield, 2006

Karnow, Stanely. *Vietnam: A History.*2nd ed. New York: Penguin Books, 1997

Knieff, Albert L. A Family of Pioneers: The Evolution of a Wilderness Farm into a Modern Community on the Shore of Bay Lake. Deerwood, MN: KSA Publishing, 1996

King, Martin Luther, Jr., "I Have a Dream," March on Washington, Lincoln Memorial, Washington, D.C., Aug. 28, 1963

Klein, Joe. Politics Lost: How American Democracy was Trivialized by People Who Think You're Stupid. New York: Doubleday, 2006

Lebedoff, David. *Ward Number Six*. New York: Scribner and Sons, 1972

Maraniss, David, They Marched into Sunlight: War and Peace, Vietnam and America, October 1967. New York: Simon & Schuster, 2003

McCullough, David. *Truman*. New York: Simon & Schuster, 1992

Murray, Stuart. *Eyewitness Vietnam War.* New York: DK Publishing, Inc., 2005

Nathanson, Iric. "Two Favorite Sons: The Humphrey-McCarthy Battle of 1968." Minnpost, May 25, 2011

Olson, James. *Dictionary of the Vietnam War*. New York: Peter Bedrick Books, 1988

Perlstein, Rick. Nixonland: The Rise of a President and the Fracturing of America New York: Simon & Schuster, 2008

Reeves, Richard. *President Kennedy: Profile of Power.*, New York: Simon & Schuster, 1993

Rosenbaum, David. "George McGovern Dies at 90, a Liberal Trounced but Never Silenced," *New York Times*, Oct. 21, 2012

Rosten, Leo. *The New Joys of Yiddish*. New York: Three Rivers Press, 2000

Schlesinger, Arthur M. *Robert Kennedy and His Times*. New York: Ballantine Books, 1978

Silverman, Morris, Rabbi. *Passover Haggadah*. Hartford, Conn: Prayer Book Press, 1959

Solberg, Carl. *Hubert Humphrey: A Biography*. New York: W.W. Norton & Company, 1984

Strand, Janice. *History of Battle Point on Bay Lake* . Bay Lake Township, MN (anthology), 2010

Tilsen, Kenneth E., Judging the Judges: Justice, Persistence, and the Minnesota Court During the War in Vietnam. St Cloud, Minn.: North Star Press of St Cloud, Inc., 2002

Van Dyk, Ted. Heroes, Hacks, and Fools: Memoirs from the Political Inside. Seattle : University of Washington Press, 2007

White, Theodore H., *The Making of the President 1968*. New York: HarperCollins, 2010ons professor at Syracuse University—who pointed a speech education graduate toward the University of Minnesota in 1956.

Acknowledgments

Special thanks to Ellen for her editing; for harnessing my play with words when needed. Her ideas helped me shape my book. I thank my niece for a project she began. In 2013 she and her grandmother created "The Life of Barbara F. Amram." The time line was the first thing that inclined me to write this memoir. A debt of gratitude is owed to religious director Sue Summit for her scanning, her proofing and cooperation on this book.

In the dim of bar light, under the weight of voices, I shared a beer as my interviews with Howard Kaibel spontaneously expired. The retired public defender and administrative judge sat looking over his glasses. He studied his New York Times, his days in politics far behind him, and apprised himself of how his "team" was doing. He smiled, laughed with a repressed fondness, and graciously answered my questions. It was a coincidence that I met him through a friend months before I began this book. He was barely twenty when he worked for Gene McCarthy with my parents. I thank him for culling his mind, like he did the New York Times, to recall days in 1968. However it always seemed he had better memories of the Civil Rights Movement, when his hero, Hubert Humphrey, was still a good guy.

I thank those—too numerous to mention—who created those memories. I was reminded of the thoughtfulness and things done out of love during six weeks I checked out of this world in the winter of 1971. I thank Donna, Marie, Yvonne, and others for their acts of kindness or words read to my unconscious ears. Finally, I mention Ray—a communications professor at Syracuse University—who pointed a speech education graduate toward the University of Minnesota in 1956.

About the Author

After graduation from the University of Minnesota in 1989, Michael P. Amram began writing prose and poetry, which was influenced by living and working in an urban environment as a disabled person. Amram's first novel *The Orthodoxy of Arrogance* was published in 2013; the manuscript of which was chosen as a finalist for the Loft Literary Center's 2011/12 Mentor Series. His poetry first appeared in the 2013 collection *Scenes the Writer Shows: Forty-one Places a Poem Can Go*. In 2015 he read his poetry at the Loft's dedication as an International Peace Site. Amram lives with his wife in Minneapolis. Visit his blog at **paulamram.blogspot.com**.